The MORALITY of Capitalism

Edited by
MARK W. HENDRICKSON

The Foundation for Economic Education, Inc.
Irvington-on-Hudson, New York

The Morality of Capitalism

Second revised edition

The Foundation for Economic Education, Inc.
30 South Broadway
Irvington-on-Hudson, NY 10533
(914) 591-7230

Publisher's Cataloging in Publication
(Prepared by Quality Books, Inc.)

The Morality of capitalism.—2nd rev. ed. / edited by
Mark W. Hendrickson
p. cm.
Includes index.
ISBN 1–57246–055-5

1. Capitalism—Moral and ethical aspects. I. Hendrickson, Mark W.

HB501.M67 1966 330.12'2
QBI96–40110

Library of Congress Catalog Card Number: 96–85563

Second revised edition, August 1996

Cover design by Beth R. Bowlby
Manufactured in the United States of America

Table of Contents

Introduction

Since the collapse of the Soviet Union the specter of totalitarianism and nuclear devastation has lost most of its terror. Communism as a political system has fallen into disrepute and many communist leaders now are extolling the virtues of democracy and the market order. The death of Soviet communism, however, has not removed many of the intellectual and moral roots from which the system has sprung. They continue to live and grow in many quarters.

The roots become clearly visible when we ponder the various versions of communism. The Soviet communism of Lenin and Stalin has collapsed spectacularly, but the communism of Karl Marx's *Communist Manifesto* is very much alive. Most people quickly reject the Soviet version with its many repugnant features, but passionately defend the *Manifesto* version which calls for "a heavy progressive or graduated income tax," for "centralization of credit in the hands of government, by means of a federal bank with federal funds and an exclusive money monopoly," "centralization of the means of communication and transport in the hands of government," "free education for all children in public schools," and other government functions. The Soviet communists have fallen silent, but the disciples of the *Manifesto* are as vocal as ever. They recite and reassert old Marxian arguments against the private-property system and at times may even add a few of their own.

Despite the visible debacle of the Soviet world, these followers reiterate the old charges of exploitation of labor by unbridled capitalism, of chronic unemployment and grinding poverty. Many disciples, especially in the United States, seek to buttress their position with ethical arguments which hopefully take priority over all matters economic. They elevate the equality of incomes to an ethical postulate and then find capitalism wanting. They fall back to an ethical-aesthetic denunciation of the profit motive and then condemn capitalism. They may even find grievous fault with a presumed lack of cultural values and cultural achievements of capitalism. Paying scant attention to the Soviet experience and lesson, they build a bastion of *concern and compassion* or even *ethical socialism* which would subject all economic activity to ethical circumspection.

It is difficult to refute or confound an ethical postulate, in particular the supposition that all men ought to have equal incomes or at least enjoy similar income levels. It is a value judgment not open to reasoning. But we may demonstrate the costs and consequences of a policy that would seek to enforce income equality. And we may show how any attempt at equalization would conflict with other postulates such as individual freedom, economic well-being, and the preservation of social peace.

The income equalizers obviously would deny individual freedom to those individuals from whom the income would be taken forcibly. They would grant special coercive powers to those officials and their agents who would seize the income and then allocate the shares to other individuals. The seizure and distribution inevitably would generate several sources of bitter conflict which by itself precludes an important ethical postulate: social harmony and peace.

Income equalization tacitly assumes that national income is a given automatism independent of any policy government may conduct. In reality, national income consists of individual incomes which are the result of individual choice, will, and effort. They are affected immediately and directly by any outside force and influence. Individuals do react to force; and even if they should act like programmed robots, much of the income they are forced to surrender may be taken from individual saving and investment and allocated to public consumption. It may be channeled from production for the future to enjoyment in the present. Government policies toward income equalization, therefore, tend to lead to future stagnation or even reduction of national income. In time, the poor members of society who were supposed to benefit from the equalization may actually sink deeper into poverty and despair. And once again, the postulate of economic equality conflicts with another postulate: the economic well-being of all members of society.

The ethical critics of the private-property order do not tire of berating the profit motive and the acquisitive instinct. They rail at successful merchants and shopkeepers, at wealthy bankers, stockbrokers, and capitalists. They rave at advertising, marketing, and other business practices designed to inform and influence people in making economic decisions. Free competition, in their belief, lacks any rule of fairness or reasonableness and, therefore, cannot be the ruling principle of the economic world. It consumes and wastes human life in a daily struggle for economic survival. It is necessary, therefore, that economic affairs be subjected to a true and effective guiding principle: ethical postulates.

It is moot to argue about the inner drive, impulse, and intention which cause a person to act in a certain way. Yet these critics of the profit motive are ever ready to cast doubt on the motives of businessmen, especially entrepreneurs and capitalists, while imputing pure and honorable motives to legislators, regulators, and tax collectors. They never explain why the men and women who manage the production process, be it the manufacturer of tennis shoes or the arranger of ragtime music, are supposed to be so different in drive and intention from politicians and public servants, many of whom have difficulties managing their own affairs. They never clarify why a businessman who cares for and waits on his fellowmen should be weighed in the balance and found wanting when compared with a legislator or regulator who prefers to rule over his fellowmen.

Ethical censors are highly critical of what they believe to be a dearth of the cultural achievements of businessmen. They deplore the loss of the fine art of living, of education, and the refining of the mind, emotions, manners, and taste. Yet, wherever they can, they favor all forms of "modern living" and support movements of progressivism and intellectualism which seek salvation in new institutions, programs, and projects. They are quick to feature the cult of man, his contemporary art, much of which is profane and vulgar, and the omnipresent state. They favor original and raw behavior and freedom from social ties. Wherever these critics come to power, however, they "elevate" society, the group, or the community to their standard of reference for social values. Placing little emphasis on man, his nature, or his personality, they busy themselves organizing, concentrating, managing, and administering society. Always making light of the loss of individual freedom, they tend to reduce man to a means toward a high-sounding end.

Society exaltation and government veneration have advanced slowly and steadily in the hearts and minds of many people and eroded their moral fiber. Many Americans now rate entitlement income and security more highly than individual freedom, self-reliance, and personal dignity. What they call "freedom" is more often than not merely license, arbitrariness, or political favor. Choice and decision-making are shifting from the individual, the family, and the group to political institutions. The power of government is growing, but the sense of community is dying. This is clearly visible in the activities of demagogues and lobbyists who are turning politics into a fine art of political burglary, channeling other people's income into the pockets of their favorite groups. All along, government is losing public esteem and moral authority, or worse, is becoming an object of contempt and corruption.

In an unhampered private-property order, government is not an almsgiver of gifts and grantor of favors but an instrumentality which protects life and property. It does not give signals of what shall be done and does not preside over economic production. It merely enforces and defends man's inalienable rights and protects him against wrongs of his fellowmen. Such an order would be preferable to a command system even if it were less productive. Fortunately, it does not call for economic disinterest and self-neglect: *the social order which safeguards the standards of ethical conduct and moral judgment is also the more productive economic order*; it releases and activates the productive forces inherent in individual self-assertion and creates a prosperous commonwealth by adapting economic policy to the nature of man rather than forcing man to adjust to policy.

Ethical considerations give essential justification to private property in the means of production, to market competition, and the profit system. They grant the capitalistic economic order an important place within a moral order, a place with one system of ethics for rulers and subjects alike—to be honest and peaceful, refraining from any action that would do harm to a fellow man. In fact, the capitalistic order gives rise to a moral system of rewards and punishment based on integrity, effort, talent, learning, and thrift. By lending protection to economic freedom it also becomes the ultimate guarantor of the noneconomic elements of freedom such as the freedom of speech, of religion, the press, personal behavior, etc.

The forces of spiritual and moral decay are besieging the capitalistic order. They are secularizing Western culture, leaving public opinion largely atheistic. Since most men cannot exist in a religious vacuum, they invent and cling to surrogate religions of all kinds, to politics and political passions, fads and cults—or they lose themselves in sport and gambling, in sexuality, rowdiness, crime, drug addiction, and many other vices.

"Modern man" is quick to point to the external conditions of human existence as fashioned by modern technology, organization, and social institutions. He is aware that there is no precedent in the known course of human history for a world population explosion and the growth of great cities we are witnessing today. There is no precedent for a single civilization reaching into all corners of the world and overshadowing all others as our Western civilization. And never before has technology affected the lives and concerns of people everywhere. He cites all these radical changes to justify the wanton insolence of an atheistic humanism which provides the raw material for the omnipresent state. Being spiritually homeless and morally adrift, man looks for surrogates in political and social "religions." At the top of his surrogate list is politics, in particular, the politics of envy and entitlement.

Atheistic humanism has a willing ally in historical relativism which maintains that the basis of judgment is relative, differing according to time and place, and in relativistic sociology which makes groups, classes, and nations the basis of its judgment. Both have gathered for an assault on the private-property order. Ethical statism is carrying the colors.

This assault is the spur to this collection of *Freeman Classics*. It suffers from an embarrassment of riches which similar anthologies rarely encounter. It had to exclude numerous brilliant articles worthy of inclusion but considerations of space narrowly limited the selection. It gives primacy to the writings of the well-known deans of the moral order of capitalism, to Edmund Opitz, Leonard E. Read, F. A. Hayek, and Israel M. Kirzner. All in all, this volume displays the scope and power of *The Freeman* way of dealing with the moral issues of our time. It reveals the vision and wisdom of a talented editor, Dr. Paul Poirot, who for more than thirty years guided *The Freeman* as the flagship publication of The Foundation for Economic Education. He arranged and orchestrated the voices heard in this anthology. May they be heard in the din of political cunning and corruption.

—HANS F. SENNHOLZ

I. THE SPIRITUAL FOUNDATION

Capitalism and Our Culture

by Edmund A. Opitz

The current revival of interest in religion in America has been variously interpreted. At the very least, it means that many of us may be disposed to re-examine the spiritual foundations on which our culture has been erected. Our heritage of free churches—religious bodies possessing an authority of their own, independent of the State—is obviously rooted in the unique intellectual and cultural soil of the West.

But we need to be reminded that our other cherished institutions spring from the same soil. Modern science, education, our tradition of limited government, and our taste for free enterprise or capitalism are all anchored to the same spiritual foundation; and, as superstructures, they are all affected by the decay or the loss of prestige of their foundation.

Shoring up this spiritual foundation directly is one thing; defending it against the indirect erosion which results from an attack on one of its autonomous offspring such as science, education, or free enterprise is another. Science and education have able defenders, so the attack on our culture often centers on economics where it sometimes achieves a semblance of plausibility. It was a unique combination of cultural factors which encouraged the emergence of capitalism, and it may be argued that the very survival of free, private enterprise depends as much on getting these cultural factors back into proper focus as it does in knowing the case for the free market.

In the philosophy underlying the practices of capitalism the market is used as a device for making economic decisions—the "market" being the pattern precipitated by the voluntary buying habits of free men and women. Men engaged in economic activity at any level may be guilty of coercion and fraud, just as they may be guilty of coercion and fraud in any other context. When this is the case,

---

The Reverend Mr. Opitz, author of the book *Religion and Capitalism: Allies, Not Enemies*, and well-known writer and lecturer, was a member of the senior staff of The Foundation for Economic Education, 1955–1992. He is a contributing editor of *The Freeman*. This article originally appeared in the March 1958 issue of *The Freeman*.

they may properly be censured for their malpractices. This is worlds apart, however, from the wholesale condemnation of the institution of the free market by collectivists, or the thoughtless criticisms of otherwise thoughtful people.

Economic activity, subject to the same ethical and institutional restraints that hedge all human actions, is no more properly subject to political invasion than is religion or science or any other human venture. Economics, moreover, occupies a strategic position among the various activities of man. Economic activity is not merely the means to material ends; it is also the means to all our ends. Thus, while it may serve on a humbler level than science, education, and religion, economics is a necessary means to these ends. If its integrity as a means to these ends is not respected, it may become the instrument to destroy them as well as to impair the spiritual foundation they rest upon.

A great social upheaval occurred several centuries ago—one of those great, deep, tidal changes in the human spirit manifesting itself on the level of society as new institutions and a new outlook on life. Different aspects of this transformation were labeled the Renaissance, the Reformation, and the Counter-Reformation, the whole affair being religious in nature. Men felt the urge to love God for himself; and, as a parallel development, to pursue truth for its own sake. This latter urge is the wellspring of the scientific method.

But like other people, specialists in science easily lapse into an attitude of unawareness of the unique spiritual and social conditions which make their specialty possible. They are "radically ignorant," writes Ortega y Gasset, of "how society and the heart of man are to be organized in order that there may continue to be investigators." And so we now have science perverted, and some scientists placing their talents at the disposal of politicians in the planned State. This is bound to happen when the metaphysical foundations of science are ignored.

Spiritual Foundations

A human culture is born as something "cultivated," something developed by education, discipline, and training. Its spiritual foundation is constructed slowly and painfully, like the building of a breakwater by throwing in bag after bag of cement until finally the top of the pile appears above water. Modern culture had been in preparation for centuries before it erupted in the sixteenth century and allowed a new outlook, a new spirit, and a new set of values to release and direct human energy. Men threw off the dead weight of ancient restraints—the various justifications for the tyrannies of political government, the controls on man's productive energy, the discouragement of efforts to investigate the natural universe.

The material prosperity we know and have known in America is a direct outgrowth of the spiritual and social upheaval which surfaced about four centuries ago. The critics of capitalism became aware of this connection at least fifty years ago when Max Weber published his enormously influential book, *The Protestant Ethic and the Spirit of Capitalism.* The revolutionaries, however, had employed this strategy much earlier. G. Zacher, in 1884, wrote in *The Red International*, "Whoever assails Christianity assails at the same time monarchy and capitalism!"

If our common Judeo-Christian heritage paved the way for the rise of capitalism, then a subtle way of causing a decline of capitalism would be to refrain from openly attacking it while concentrating on weakening the foundation which holds it up. This would kill two birds with one stone, in the manner advised by the French revolutionist two centuries ago who said, "Don't attack the monarch, attack the *idea* of monarchy."

Perhaps the importance of the spiritual and cultural foundation of the West may best be illustrated by comparison between the Oriental and the Western scene. A traveler in the Orient is struck immediately by the amount of human muscle power still used to do the heavy work of society. The streets of an Indian city are crowded with men carrying things, pushing things, and acting as beasts of burden. The strong impression which these scenes evoke is that the Orient needs machines so that horsepower can relieve manpower. [Ed. note: There has been great progress in some Asian countries—those which have practiced capitalism—since these words were written in 1958.]

Questions and Answers

Why doesn't the Orient have the machines which would lighten human toil? Is she too poor to buy them? So was Europe a few centuries ago; and then the energies of Europeans poured out and channeled themselves in patterns of relief from much of the backbreaking toil which is still the fate of their brothers in the Far East.

Might it be that the people of the Orient are not bright enough to invent and build their own machines? To the contrary, many of her people are bursting with creative energy, and they have inventive minds, as witness their philosophies, their arts, their handicrafts. And rich natural resources are available to them.

Perhaps the Oriental society has been shackled by its prevailing forms of despotic government. There *has* been despotism in the Orient, native and foreign; but the questions arise: Why have people over the centuries quietly consented to submit to tyranny? Why has the idea of limited government gained so little foothold among them? Why doesn't the Orient invent the machines, embrace the technology, and set up the industries which would provide the goods and lighten the burdens that now lie so heavily on the backs of half a billion people?

These are questions that cannot be answered on the level of technology or on the level of political and social organization. The answers must be sought at those deeper levels where vital decisions are made which permit or repress the emergence of a belief in the dignity of man, and in freedom, and in such of its natural corollaries as science and technology. Natural resources and opportunities are of secondary importance; what is of primary importance is the possession of a religious heritage—or an attitude toward the universe—which encourages men to take hold of natural opportunities. This heritage Europe had in the Judeo-Christian tradition in which was embodied elements of Greek culture—the whole being called Christendom. When that tradition came to renewed life at the dawn of the modern era, it was the fountainhead of great changes in Western society. Population increased many times; simultaneously the well-being of individuals increased. Famines disappeared; some diseases were eliminated altogether, and the ravages of others were mitigated. Education spread to the outermost edges of society. During the same period of modern history Oriental society has been virtually static—until the ferment of the last few years.

Equal Before God

At the heart of the great Western upheaval was the idea that the individual worshiper could come into the presence of God without the mediation of any special class of men, or of any group, or of any nation. According to this faith, the Creator and Sustainer of life, the Lord of the universe, is nevertheless, and paradoxically, close to every person and interested in the most humble.

Think what this belief, strongly held, would do for the humble who walked the earth, how it would straighten their backbones and lift their chins! Think what this belief would do to tyranny. If every man thought of himself as the creature of God and potentially God's child, he certainly would not long submit to being the creature of any other man or of any group of men or of any government! No longer could it be regarded as right, or as the will of God, that any man be placed at the disposal of any other man or group. Thus, every person was conceived to have "rights" which no one should impair, and out of this came a concept of government as a social institution set up voluntarily by men to secure each of them in his "rights."

We are proud, and rightly so, of the experiment in government set in motion on these shores a little more than two centuries ago. Perhaps the keynote of this new kind of government was struck by James Madison in his thirty-ninth Federalist Paper when he wrote of the determination "to rest all our political experiments on the capacity of mankind for self-government." This cannot be construed to mean that Madison suffered from any illusions as to the utopian possibilities locked up in the average human breast. But for the first time in history the individual person was not to be a creature of government or its minions. Inherent rights were lodged in each person as his natural endowment from God, and the exercise of his individual energies was strictly a matter of his own business—until he trespassed on the rights of other individuals.

In the American scheme, men had a larger measure of political liberty than men had ever had before, and they obtained their measure of freedom by limiting government to taking care of the one interest men have in common—the removal of barriers to the peaceful exercise and exchange of human energy.

The American concept of government did not spring into being full blown from a few brains; it was hammered out in the course of long experience and debate. By the middle of the eighteenth century Americans were protesting that the exactions of the British crown were violating their rights as men, whereas but a generation earlier they had demanded their rights as Englishmen. A revolution in thought and outlook separates the former concept from the latter. In drawing the lines of battle on their rights as Englishmen, the colonists had in mind the concessions which their ancestors, beginning with the barons at Runnymede, had wrung from their sovereigns. In standing on their rights as men, the colonists drew upon another dimension, the theological. This is probably what de Tocqueville had in mind in 1835 when he wrote of Americans that "religion . . . is the first of their political institutions."

Religious Aspects of Political Liberty

When religious considerations are introduced into political theory, government is ideally limited to securing the ends of liberty and justice for all men alike. Political liberty thus has spiritual antecedents, and it serves spiritual ends by providing the social conditions which enable persons to achieve the goals appropriate to human nature.

Political liberty also serves man's creaturely needs. Under political liberty a certain pattern of economic activity emerges, properly called "capitalism." There is no more warrant in common sense or in theory for fettering men's economic activities than there is for arbitrarily curtailing his scientific, educational, or religious activities. But by constant repetition of untruths and halftruths, it has been made to appear that every ill from which our society suffers is due to freedom of economic enterprise, whereas the real cause of many of these ills is actually the result of the impairments of that freedom.

In recent years, business and industry have gone through the wringer. Businessmen, who are as good and as bad as any other group of men, have been singled out for special treatment. Industry as a whole has been tied down with a network of laws and controls. While some branches of it were treated to special privileges by government, other branches suffered from political discrimination.

During this same period a new conception of government has gained popularity. It is the very concept against which eighteenth-century Americans protested and fought—the concept that government is the seat of ultimate power in society and therefore possesses all the rights which it dispenses provisionally to people as political expedience dictates. Thus, the older American concept of the relation of government and people is turned inside out.

Whenever men have yielded to the lust for power and the greed for possessions, there have always been impairments of political and economic liberty of great or less degree. In the past when the going got rough, men pulled in their belts, grumbled, and consoled each other with the literature of freedom, sacred and secular. They were sustained by their faith that those who loved liberty were on the side of the right, and that the right would eventually triumph. They might perish, but their principles would outlast any tyrant. But now the situation is different. Values have been transvalued, and impairments of political and economic liberty are made on principle. Thus the blows struck at limited government and free enterprise do not stop after doing their damage there. They go deeper and strike at the spiritual and cultural bases of our society, at that substratum of our life which we, until recently, have so taken for granted.

In our present situation, the most immediately oppressive things seem to emanate from an overgrown, bureaucratic government. Merely to remove these restraints and directives is of little use, however, if we leave intact the *concept* of omnipotent government—or the seeds of this concept—to spawn more restrictions. An erroneous idea of government must be replaced by a correct idea. But when we seek to refurbish the American idea of limited government, we find that originally the concept stemmed from a spiritual foundation which is itself badly in need of rehabilitation. It is at this fundamental level that the most intensive work needs to be done. But because so few people are aware of the importance of this level, almost no one is working at it. Unless this spiritual foundation is rehabilitated, work at the less profound levels cannot endure, touching as it does only the margins of the problem.

Capitalism and Morality

by Edward Coleson

"Nothing is more unpopular today than the free market economy, i.e., capitalism. Everything that is considered unsatisfactory in present day conditions is charged to capitalism." Thus wrote Ludwig von Mises in 1947.[1] But the bad reputation of capitalism is of long standing. John Ruskin denounced Adam Smith as ". . . the half-breed and half-witted Scotchman who taught the deliberate blasphemy: 'Thou shalt hate the Lord, thy God, damn his law, and covet thy neighbor's goods.'"[2] Marxists and Fabian Socialists have built up a large library of anti-capitalist propaganda over the years.

In times of economic crisis the opposition to capitalism becomes even more pronounced. During the Great Depression, in a book co-authored by a number of prominent churchmen, we were told: "The whole future of Christian societies depends on whether Christianity, or rather Christians, decisively leave off supporting capitalism and social injustice. . . ."[3] Such pronouncements could be cited almost without number. In the recent past it was assumed that the more orthodox and evangelical wing of the Christian movement was more kindly disposed toward capitalism, and there is statistical evidence to support this view; but now a group of exceedingly vocal evangelicals have appeared who denounce this traditional economic and political conservatism as un-Christian.

It would appear to me that one of our most urgent tasks is to try to understand this bitter animosity against capitalism by men of intelligence, social concern, and even Christian faith. Certainly, part of these socialistic and communistic dissenters have a vested interest in the destruction of capitalism and our nation, too. Yet many are honest men of good will who oppose a market economy because they fail to understand it.

Dr. Coleson, a frequent contributor to *The Freeman*, was for many years professor of economics at Spring Arbor College in Michigan. He is now retired and lives in Puerto Rico.
This article originally appeared in the October 1973 issue of *The Freeman*.

No Pre-Industrial Utopia

In point of time, the first fallacy to contend with is the pre-capitalist state of society. It is easy to dream up an idyllic and utopian age when unspoiled peasants lived life to the full close to nature, a medieval version of Rousseau's "Noble Savage" in a primitive paradise. Actually, Hobbes' insistence that life in a state of nature was "nasty, brutish and short" is closer to the truth. Adam Smith mentions that in his time, "It is not uncommon . . . in the Highlands of Scotland for a mother who has borne twenty children not to have two alive."[4] Remember, as Warren Thompson tells us in *Population Problems*, this was as recent as two centuries ago. Another writer tells us that "the deaths in all medieval towns largely exceeded the births, so that the towns only survived by constant recruitment from the country. . . ." Famines were frequent and severe. More recently, E. A. Wrigley claims that in certain French parishes, which he studied in detail, the death rate was proportional to the price of grain back nearly three centuries ago.[5] And pollution—you should have seen and smelt it—back when everything was thrown into the streets. The preindustrial state of affairs was no paradise, even if conditions did not improve as fast as they should have as we moved into the modern period. The contention that everything was lovely until the vicious capitalist played the serpent to that Eden is not supported by the facts of history.

Another notion is that life was relatively simple in the pre-capitalistic social and political order. The reasoning is as follows: life was simpler in the 1890s than it is today and—by an extension of the same logic—it must have been even more simple in the 1690s or 1590s. Wrong again. Life was relatively simple in the late Victorian period as a few surviving oldsters still remember; but the 1690s were as much like today as a preindustrial society could be. As one example, in France "it took more than two thousand pages to print the rules established for the textile industry between 1666 and 1730."[6] Punishment for breaking these regulations was severe. Multitudes of people died for economic offenses that ought never to have been considered crimes. And, remember, all of this happened before the Industrial Revolution made life complicated—or so we are told. It should be obvious that this complexity grew, not out of the necessities of the situation—what did they need of thousands of pages of textile "codes" in the days of hand-weavers—but out of a philosophy of government. As has been said, the men of that age "displayed a marked belief in the efficacy of government to achieve any and all desired ends by means of legislation."[7] How modern!

Adam Smith and the Rule of Law

Another common idea is that Adam Smith was an anarchist. Nowadays if one admits that he believes in free enterprise, he is often reminded that we must have government. There are many anarchists in our midst today and it appears their numbers are increasing—perhaps a reaction to the excesses of statism—but anarchy is not a necessary alternative to total government control. Smith distinguished between what he called "the laws of justice" and the inane attempts of various pressure groups to rig the market in favor of their petty interests.[8] To Smith the task of government was the administration of justice, not the job of running everybody's business. He also thought the government should protect the nation from foreign invasion and maintain "certain public works and certain public institutions" for the general welfare, apparently services hard to charge for, such as the use of a lighthouse or the street and sidewalk in front of your house. It is obvious that Smith believed in government, but thought, like Thomas Jefferson, that it should be a "simple, frugal affair." Many people today are turning again to those two classics of 1776, *The Wealth of Nations* and the Declaration of Independence. Let's hope that limited government is coming back into fashion.

Capitalism and Greed

Another common fallacy is the idea that Adam Smith sanctified greed, that free enterprise is brutal—"every man for himself and the devil take the hindmost." Again, this has been a common view, held by both capitalists and socialists. However, this was not Smith's version of capitalism. This misconception has no doubt been the most damaging to free enterprise of all the accusations leveled against the system: both Christians and humanitarians denounce it as evil and vicious. Henry Thomas Buckle, an English historian of the last century, made an interesting observation on this problem. He pointed out that in his earlier book, *The Theory of Moral Sentiments*, Smith emphasized sympathy, and then seventeen years later he published *The Wealth of Nations* dedicated to the proposition that ". . . the great moving power of all men, all interests and all classes, in all ages and in all countries, is selfishness." This is the common view, except that most people do not know about his earlier devotion to compassion. Buckle described what appeared to be a dramatic change in Smith's outlook:

> In this way Adam Smith completely changes the premises he had assumed in his earlier work. Here, he makes men naturally selfish; formerly, he had made them naturally sympathetic. Here, he represents them pursuing wealth for sordid objects. . . . It now appears that benevolence and affection have no influence over our actions. Indeed, Adam Smith will hardly admit humanity into his theory of motives.[9]

Since Buckle considered *The Wealth of Nations* as "probably the most important book which has ever been written," he seems to have had no prejudice against its author. He explains the apparent inconsistency, the obvious shift in philosophical position, by saying that Smith was investigating both sides of the same problem, that the books were "compensatory rather than hostile," that one supplemented the other, that we all have a streak of sympathy and also of selfishness in our make-up. Whatever Smith's intent, the image of greed has come through to the general public. However, I suspect that the people who talk the loudest about the problem have never read *The Wealth of Nations.*

One of our contemporaries, Richard C. Cornuelle, has also tried to resolve the dilemma. He begins with Mandeville's familiar *Fable of the Bees,* published in 1705, a satire written to prove "Private Vices make Public Benefits," as the subtitle tells us. The question was whether the individual man's greed did or did not promote the general welfare by increasing economic activity and hence the standard of living for everybody. The older view was that no one could gain except at other people's loss, that we can only enrich ourselves by impoverishing others. As Cornuelle tells us,

> Mandeville merely stated the "private vices—public benefits" dilemma. It was left to Adam Smith to resolve it. In his monumental

> *Wealth of Nations*, he told the world clearly and comprehensively what made commerce work. There is an astonished tone in his work, as if he could hardly believe his own discoveries. . . .[10]

Smith had discovered to his amazement that the true long-range self-interest of each individual was compatible with everyone else's welfare, that what was good for one was best for all. If this is true, there is no necessary conflict between Adam Smith's earlier philosophical system founded on sympathy and the alleged greed of *The Wealth of Nations*. As Smith said, the businessman in seeking his own interest is "led by an invisible hand" to promote the general welfare, "an end which was no part of his intention."[11] This is an attractive idea: what is good for the farmer is good for the consumer, what is good for labor is good for management, what is good for Russia, Red China, Cuba, and our friendlier neighbors is good for the United States and vice versa. This sounds great, but is it true?

If we assume that what is good for each is good for all, the next question is whether we will automatically know what is right and spontaneously do it. Of course, we need to differentiate between blind greed and enlightened self-interest, but even then there is little historical evidence to support the view that we will necessarily know the right and do it. Unfortunately, there was a tendency after the publication of *The Wealth of Nations* to assume that if businessmen "did what came naturally" that the consequences would surely be good.

It should be remembered that about the time Adam Smith was born Newton captured the popular imagination with his famous solution of the riddle of the universe, the so-called "Newtonian synthesis" of the astronomy and physics since 1543, the work of Copernicus, Kepler and Galileo. As a consequence, it became the fashion to look for mechanical laws of human behavior, of society, of government, and of the life of man in every dimension. Men had become machines. Malthus' famous essay of 1798 warned that population would automatically outrun any possible increase in the supply of food so that no improvement in the human condition would be possible. Little wonder that he and his good friend Ricardo earned for economics the nickname, that "dismal science."

English Reform and Free Trade

If a few intellectuals were prepared to let Nature take its course back then, the "do-nothing" social policy so often associated in the popular view with laissez faire, certainly there was no lack of reform efforts before and after 1800. It was during these decades that William Wilberforce and the Clapham Sect were laboring mightily for the abolition of slavery. It was really not a good time to push reform either, since the French Revolution began in 1789 and the world was not done with Napoleon until after Waterloo in 1815. While the conflict was not continuous for this quarter of a century, wars and rumors of wars were the rule. In spite of the turmoil, Wilberforce and his associates got the English share of the slave trade (the transportation of slaves from Africa to the Americas) outlawed in 1807. After the Napoleonic Wars the British government and the Royal Navy worked diligently to suppress the commerce in slaves altogether and pressured other governments into cooperating. After the Civil War, with its Emancipation Proclamation plus the abolition of slavery in the Latin American nations to the south of us about the same time, it appeared that the future of human freedom was secure. Reform had paid off.

During the long decades of the struggle against slavery there were those who argued eloquently that the best thing to do about slavery was to ignore the problem; maybe it would go away of itself. Indeed, it may seem a paradox that Englishmen who were going laissez faire in economics should at the same time have been working diligently to suppress slavery far from their shores and in lands where they had no jurisdiction. It would have seemed logical for them to have tended to their own business, the job of making money, and to have let slavery "wither away."

This is an exceedingly important point. The English reformers of the early and middle nineteenth century were not anarchists. They believed in freedom under law—God's Law—and since slavery was clearly contrary to God's Law, they were working for its abolition. It would certainly be a revolution today if all laws and political arrangements that had no moral justification should be abolished. Perhaps we have grown too tolerant of the powers that be. The Nazi and Communist oppression of the last half century has shown that power corrupts, that progress is not inevitable, and that freedom is not automatic.

The great English reform effort of the last century is misunderstood and largely forgotten, yet their accomplishments were enormous. According to Earle E. Cairns' account in *Saints and Society*, Wilberforce and his associates accomplished more of a constructive nature than any reform movement in history. It was out of this context that Victorian free trade and free enterprise came, and the leaders of the movement which made it happen were devout Christians who regarded their campaign as a holy crusade. Before free trade became a popular issue, the British had abolished plantation slavery in their colonies (Wilberforce died as the abolition bill was being debated in Parliament in 1833, but lived long enough to know it would pass); to many Englishmen free trade and free enterprise were just the next logical national objectives. In one of the first lectures delivered under the auspices of the fledgling free trade movement ". . . it was stated that the organization was established on the same righteous principle as the Anti-Slavery Society."[12] Although everyone recognized that these were economic questions, the posture of righteousness and reform was maintained throughout the campaign.

Repeal of the Corn Laws

The focus of the economic reformers' attention was the "British farm program," the famous Corn Laws, a complicated system of tariffs which was devised to keep out foreign grain until domestic prices became prohibitive. To Richard Cobden, John Bright, and other members of the Anti-Corn Law League, this practice of keeping food needlessly scarce and expensive was criminal and wicked, and no amount of legislation would make it moral. Even that distinguished reformer Lord Ashley, the seventh Earl of Shaftesbury, a landed aristocrat who had nothing to gain and perhaps much to lose if English markets were flooded with America's agricultural abundance, voted for free trade in food because it was right. By contrast, those of us who remember forty years of Federal farm programs since Henry Wallace "plowed under cotton and killed little pigs" in the spring of 1933, recall little attempt to approach the problem ethically. Such was not the thinking of the early Victorians. A great conference of the clergy was held at

Manchester and many ministers began to preach that the Corn Laws were "anti-scriptural and anti-religious, opposed to the law of God." The League produced and distributed many tons of propaganda leaflets. It has even been claimed "that there was not one literate person in all of Great Britain who had not read of the League and its work by the end of 1844,"[13] a degree of saturation it would be hard to achieve even today.

This enormous effort paid off. By 1846, the League succeeded in abolishing the hated Corn Laws, and a flood of cheap grain from America inundated the British (and later Western European) markets and provided the common working man with a decent diet at a reasonable price. In the next few years the British abolished their remaining tariffs, which their neighbors tended to do also. The stage was set for the enormous growth of world trade in the late Victorian period, a burst of creative activity which promoted prosperity and economic development around the world and in the United States, too. Their faith in freedom was not ill-founded. The English free traders were optimists who "were much embarrassed . . . by the dismal parts of the dismal science," as expounded a generation earlier by Malthus and Ricardo. They "avidly seized upon the purified version of economics presented by the Frenchman, Frederic Bastiat."[14] These men believed that progress and peace were the fruits of a proper economic policy, and in the short run, at least, this seemed to be the case. Those in our midst who are oppressed and depressed by the strife, turmoil, and seemingly permanent poverty of vast areas of the world today, would do well to study the Victorian example.

Then and Now

Certainly, these men and their times make an interesting topic for study, particularly the contrasts between then and today. As one author says, ". . . in the early nineteenth century the upper middle-class elite believed in piety, reform of Church and State, moral action and laissez-faire economics."[15] When comparing their day and their reform efforts with our own, the historian of the future will, if he is fair, say of them, "Never did so few accomplish so much with so little." Of our massive multi-billion-dollar attempts at remaking the world in our own time he must say, "Never did so many accomplish so little with so much."

Perhaps capitalism has much more to offer than we have realized for a long, long time. With socialist schemes collapsing all about us, it is time that we try to understand how it worked.

Faith and Freedom

It is easy to dismiss favorable comments on Victorian economic policy as procapitalist propaganda, and there is some of that along with a flood of the socialist variety. One of the most glowing evaluations of free trade and free enterprise that I have ever seen was written by an Austrian socialist, Karl Polanyi, a few years ago. He tells us that "the self-regulating market . . . produced an unheard-of material welfare."[16] As if this were not a sufficient achievement, he says, "The nineteenth century produced a phenomenon unheard of in the annals of Western civilization, namely, a hundred's years' peace—1815–1914," from Waterloo to the "Guns of August" in 1914. (I should hasten to add that he is aware of the Crimean War and the Franco-Prussian conflict but he regards them as fairly minor disturbances. The Civil War, of course, was in America, not Europe.)

After this panegyric on capitalism, a tribute as much in superlatives as Hazlitt or Mises might manage in their most enthusiastic moments, Polanyi then warns us that the market economy ". . . would have physically destroyed man and transformed his surroundings into a wilderness." What frightens him about freedom is what people might do, and have done, when you turn them loose. When one ponders the history of freedom from the days of the Roman Republic to the present, he realizes that Polanyi's fears are not unfounded. In other words, there is only freedom over time for highly responsible and moral people. Free markets and free governments must be based on solid ethical foundations, a point that Edmund Burke saw clearly in the early days of the French Revolution:

> Men are qualified for civil liberty in exact proportion to their disposition to put moral chains upon their own appetites . . . society cannot exist unless a controlling power upon will and appetite be placed somewhere, and the less of it there is within, the more there is without. It is ordained in the eternal constitution of things that men of intemperate minds cannot be free. Their passions forge their fetters.

1. Ludwig von Mises, *Planned Chaos* (Irvington-on-Hudson, N.Y.: The Foundation for Economic Education, 1977), p. 17.
2. Robert B. Downs, *Books that Changed the World* (New York: Dutton, 1956), p. 43.
3. E. Stanley Jones *et al.*, *Christian Message for the World Today* (Salem, N.H.: Ayer Co., 1977). The quotation from Chapter II, page 45, was apparently written by Basil Mathews.
4. Adam Smith, *The Wealth of Nations* (Indianapolis, Ind.: Liberty Press, 1981), p. 97.
5. E. A. Wrigley, *Population and History* (New York: Cambridge University Press, 1989), p. 66.
6. John Chamberlain, *The Roots of Capitalism* (Indianapolis, Ind.: Liberty Press, 1966), p. 20.
7. John M. Ferguson, *Landmarks of Economic Thought* (New York: Longmans, Green, and Co., 1938), p. 36.
8. Smith, p. 720.
9. Henry Thomas Buckle, *History of Civilization in England* (London: Oxford University Press, 1925–31), Vol. II, pp. 340–354.
10. Richard C. Cornuelle, *Reclaiming the American Dream* (New Brunswick, N.J.: Transaction Publishers, 1993), pp. 47–48.
11. Smith, p. 456.
12. George Barnett Smith, *The Life and Speeches of the Right Hon. John Bright, M.P.*, Vol. I, p. 133.
13. Dean Russell, *Frederic Bastiat: Ideas and Influence* (Irvington-on-Hudson, N.Y.: The Foundation for Economic Education, 1969), p. 66.
14. *Ibid.*, p. 69.
15. Robert Langbaum (Ed.), *The Victorian Age* (Chicago: Academy Chicago Publishers Ltd., 1983), p. 9.
16. Karl Polanyi, *The Great Transformation* (Boston: Beacon Press, 1957), pp. 3–5.

The Armor of Saul

by John K. Williams

One of the most dramatic stories in the Bible is the story of David and Goliath. Goliath, almost ten feet tall, was truly a fearsome figure. Every morning and every evening he, the champion of the militant Philistines, hurled his challenge at the Israelite army: Send one man out to do battle against me! If the representative of the Israelites won, the Philistines would become slaves of the Israelites. If he, Goliath, won, the Israelites would become slaves of the Philistines.

David, a mere stripling of a lad, approached his king. He claimed experience in battle—had he not, when caring for his father's sheep, actually killed a lion and a bear? Was he not therefore qualified to take on the giant?

Moved, perhaps, by the simplicity of the boy, King Saul agreed. David could fight Goliath. Indeed, David could do so wearing the king's armor. Yet, having put on the armor, the lad decided to remove it and return it to Saul. It was too heavy and impeded his movements. The armor of Saul would have hindered, not helped.

David's courage was exceeded only by his wisdom. If he were to have a chance of victory, he could not afford to do battle weighed down by unnecessary armor. Taking on the giant was courageous; to do so encumbered by the armor of Saul would be folly.

Many defenders of the freedom philosophy lack the wisdom of the youthful David. They do battle weighed down by the equivalent of Saul's armor. They allow themselves to be burdened by that which hinders rather than helps their cause. They clutter their case by accepting propositions that have nothing to do with the free society or the free market.

"We should go back to the free market"

To defend the suggestion that we should go *back* to the free market is to assume a historical claim that in itself can alienate

---

The Reverend Dr. John Williams, popular author, lecturer, and philosopher, was a resident scholar at FEE in 1985. He continues to carry the banner for liberty in his native Australia. This article originally appeared in the February 1983 issue of *The Freeman*.

men and women. It suggests retreat. It conjures up a picture. The picture is that once upon a time economic liberty was the norm. Over the years humanity moved in new directions, initiating and bringing to birth a novel experiment in economics. Central planners would coordinate and direct what hitherto had been uncoordinated and directionless. While it may be true that a defective clock *should* have its "hands turned back" so they indicate the correct time, "turning the clock back" is an activity men and women do not warm to. They tend to side with those who valiantly push forward into new and uncharted territory. Those urging that wc "go back" to the tried and the tested are perceived as cautious, indeed, perhaps somewhat nostalgic in disposition.

The truth is, of course, that those enthused by the arguing for the free market in a free society have sided with advance. The economy planned and directed by "experts" has, historically, been the norm. Monarchs knew what was best for their subjects and told them what to do. Feudal lords knew what was best for their serfs and directed their activities. Aristocrats knew what was best for the masses and dictated how these lesser mortals should spend their days.

Consider the France of Louis XIV. Every person had his or her place in society and kept to that place. The economy was carefully planned. State officials decided what industries should be established and where in France or its colonies they should be located. Imports and exports were carefully regulated. Prices were set by political figures. Governmental committees prescribed what patterns were to be woven in the State-owned tapestry works at Aubusson; indeed four long years of negotiation preceded the giving of permission to introduce "backwarp" into fabrics. Some two thousand pages were required to list the rules and regulations which were passed between 1666 and 1730 controlling the textile industry. The contemporary socialist would have been perfectly at home in such an environment!

It is the socialist, not the advocate of liberty, who yearns for the past! The Welfare State is fast regressing to Louis XIV's France. In February 1982 a special report was presented to the U.K. Parliament. Entitled *Administrative Forms in Government*, it documented the burgeoning of government forms and leaflets in Great Britain. The two thousand pages of rules and regulations governing but one industry in France three centuries ago are modest in comparison! Over 2,000 million government forms and leaflets are used by the U.K. public annually—that means thirty-six forms for every man, woman, and child in the country! The forms, as befits government, are difficult to follow and fill out; "error rates of over 30 percent, either by [government officials] or the public, are common." The report concludes by listing ten further "reports on forms" which people with nothing better to do can read.

Political Control the Norm

Political control of a nation's economy has been the usual state of affairs. The eighteenth-century lovers of liberty were the radicals. They attacked the remnants of feudalism, fought for the abolition of caste and privilege; battled for an extension of property rights so the powerful could no longer plunder at whim; agitated against entrenched, State-granted monopolies and protective tariffs which benefited the few but impoverished the many; and dreamed of an economic order controlled not by the edicts of government but by the uncoerced endeavors of the multitudes, freely producing and exchanging whatsoever goods they chose.

And they won! A hitherto unknown phenomenon emerged: sustained economic growth. In 1780 over 80 percent of French citizens spent 90 percent of their income on just sufficient bread to stay alive. In 1800 average life expectancy was, in France, twenty-seven years for females and twenty-four for males. The vast multitudes in Europe and North America labored long and hard to survive. Recurrent famines were taken for granted. But matters changed. The working populace of England quadrupled between 1800 and 1900. Real *per capita* disposable income doubled between 1800 and 1850, and doubled again between 1850 and 1900. This 1600 percent increase in available goods and services transformed the very nature of poverty, and what had once been luxuries enjoyed by the few became everyday realities possessed by nearly all.

Yet there were those who yearned for the past. There were those who wanted to turn back the clock. There were those who wanted to use the guns of government to guarantee continued possession of their wealth rather than to have that continued possession contingent upon the use of that wealth in ways which best and most efficiently satisfied the needs and desires of others. Even though they sought to lead nations back to the seventeenth and eighteenth centuries they had the impertinence to call themselves "progressives." They spoke of a yearning for a "new" socialist society—yet in truth their yearning was but nostalgia for the past.

The lover of liberty is not urging anyone to "go back" to ancient ways. He rather urges men and women to go forward, knowing not where the creativity unleashed by the free market in the free society will take them. To speak of "going back" to the free market is to weigh oneself down with the armor of Saul.

"While less moral than socialism, capitalism is more productive"

How frequently lovers of liberty concede that their opponents are idealists. "Yes, I admire your ideals. Yet they are impractical. The market works. We must be realists!"

What is so moral or idealistic about socialism? Even in purely material terms, what is moral about the inability of the 30 percent of the workforce of Russia involved in agriculture to feed a nation which once exported grain, whereas the mere 4 percent of the workforce of the United States involved in agriculture feed an entire people and a great deal of the rest of the world as well? What is so moral about the fact that the real wages of Soviet industrial workers attained the level of 1913 only in 1963?[1] What is so moral about the fact that many African States such as Tanzania which once boasted thriving agricultural bases listened to the advice of Western intellectuals consumed by a pathological hatred of the very system that had delivered them from penury, collectivized (in the name of "agrarian reform") agriculture, and now are dependent upon foreign aid for the most basic of foodstuffs? Is not the "new French" philosopher Jean François Revel correct when he suggests that these "Western experts" should "contemplate the stare of dying children looking . . . out of those pictures [from the Third World]"[2] and commune with their consciences?

Yet the moral issues run deeper. The market economy ultimately reduces to a very simple reality. Person A is skilled at catching fish. Person B is skilled at growing bananas. Person A would prefer to surrender some of his fish and secure several bananas, and person B would prefer to surrender some of his bananas and secure several fish. So they swap! Each person surrenders what he values less and acquires what he values more. Each gains. Neither loses.

Yet suppose a third person, C, enters the picture. He uses or threatens to use force and makes A give some fish to B and to himself. B and C have gained, but poor old A has lost. *The coerced exchange does not and cannot benefit all.*

When the State forgets that its task is simply to prevent people using actual or threatened force, theft, or fraud to acquire material goods, and starts deciding who "deserves" what and uses force to impose this "deserved distribution," there are losers. In spite of socialists' fantasies, the "winners" are *not* usually the poor. (Even if the poor *were* the "winners" the use of violence to take goods from those who produced them would still be immoral, but maybe the socialist could quiet his conscience by seeking refuge in the principle grasped by most evil-doers: "The end justifies the means.") Yet in truth most "transfers" of wealth, direct and indirect, tend to favor the powerful, not the poor. Tariffs, agricultural price support schemes, subsidies to health (most of which go to the medical profession), housing subsidies, subsidies to higher education—these do not benefit the poor. They hurt the poor and benefit the powerful! Then, of course, there remains the massive army of administrators, bureaucrats, and welfare workers presiding over the system: they most certainly benefit but can hardly be called "poor."

The Welfare State

Most socialists, of course, concede that the "bureaucracy has got out of hand." *Their* new and untried version of socialism will guard against this happening. Yet Ludwig von Mises saw, nearly four decades ago, that a burgeoning bureaucracy inevitably emerges in a Welfare State.[3] The reason is simple. In the market, individuals engaging in voluntary exchanges can only promote their own interests by furthering the interests of others. In the world of politics, however, this is not true. *How can the politician further his own interests?* The answer is clear: by transferring wealth to organized special interest groups! He can concentrate benefits, but disperse costs. Ordinary citizens simply cannot afford the time to dig out information as to where their taxes go. Hence powerful groups "win" and powerless individuals "lose." And to administer the transfers more bureaucrats are required. The class of net tax recipients keeps growing; the class of net tax payers keeps shrinking.

The "law of the jungle" emerges. The voluntary, peaceful exchanges of the market are supplanted by the struggle to get to the government trough. One special interest group turns in anger on another which received "better treatment." Just how "moral" is this divisive exercise of power to grab a share of what was stolen in the first place?

"Ah! But we socialists dislike selfishness. The free market enshrines it!"

The word "selfishness" is a slippery word. "Self-interest" is maybe better. Best of all, perhaps, is reference to an individual's vision of the "good life" and his attempts to realize it. In a free society all are at liberty to formulate their own such visions and strive, non-coercively, to realize them. One man may desire a modest—indeed frugal—way of life with plenty of leisure to bask in the sun, gaze in delight at the beauties of the physical world, and think. Another may dream of amassing great wealth. Each is at liberty to pursue what he desires. Yet the allegedly "selfish" man—the one who seeks great wealth—can only do so by providing other people with what they desire at least cost to these people.

Adam Smith, in 1776, spoke of the "mean rapacity" of some "merchants and manufacturers" and, perhaps unkindly, claimed that such people "seldom meet together, even for merriment and diversion, but the conversation ends in a conspiracy against the publick."[4] That was precisely why he yearned for the free market in a free society. Limited by the rule of law, "mean" and "rapacious" people would have to serve the public if they were to improve their own situations. Indeed if one asks what political and economic structures are so designed that thoroughly despicable human beings, enjoying political or economic success, are least able to hurt their fellows, the answer can only be "the free society and the free market."

Accepting the view that socialists are moral idealists, whereas those holding to the freedom philosophy are pragmatic realists, is to go into battle weighed down by the armor of Saul.

"Really, profits are very low. Successful businesses and corporations are not too greedy!"

A major company recently ran an advertisement showing the "breakdown" of the "corporation dollar." Of the total, 95¢ went in salaries, wages, the costs of raw materials, and so on. *Only 5¢ represented "profits"!* Of that amount, 3¢ were plowed back into the corporation to purchase the machinery and equipment to provide one new job (the cost of which was in excess of $30,000) and 2¢ went to shareholders.

Now I sympathize with this advertisement. A recent survey revealed that most Australians believe corporations earn an after-tax profit of "about 40 percent." A 1975 poll conducted by the U.S. Opinion Research Corporation revealed that most Americans estimate that manufacturers enjoy an after-tax profit of 33 percent. Indeed, Australian newspapers—and I would guess most U.S. and U.K. newspapers—rarely use the word "profits" without an adjective preceding it: "obscene profits," "huge profits," "record profits," and so on.

Yet, while sympathetic, I reject the advertisement and what it represents. What does it "represent"? An apology! An acceptance of the view that "profits" are somehow unpleasant or evil! Such an apology, and such an acceptance, are but part of the cumbersome armor of Saul.

Profits are good. They are "good" for shareholders, but also "good" for countless other people. How the supporter of the freedom philosophy is to explain this to his neighbors who think otherwise is difficult to determine, *but the way is most certainly not to reinforce widespread error.*

Perhaps the first point to notice is the sheer silliness of a slogan which, in Australia, adorns many a bumper bar: "People before profits!" This slogan is but a "catchy" variant of an older slogan: "Production for use, not production for profit."

The humble reality is that the person who produces goods or provides services people do not value is not going to make any profits at all! Really, that's all there is to say on this matter. After all, having pointed out that 1 + 1 = 2, there is little point in discussing the matter further. Unless, of course, like A. N. Whitehead and Bertrand Russell who, in their *Principia Mathematica*,[5] went to great lengths to explore the hidden logical subtleties of what, to the ordinary man, is self-evident, one wishes to do the same in economics. Indeed, Ludwig von Mises did just that in his masterpiece, *Human Action.*[6] Yet, for ordinary purposes, it is sufficient to point out that a company producing a commodity which people, in their fickleness or even good taste, do not wish to possess is *not* going to record massive profits!

I have no doubt that the Packard was a fine car. The American people, however, did not like it. Other companies made cars which the public preferred. Quite apart from any other consideration, the Packard was dearer than alternatives which performed just as well. So the people said "No, thank you" to the manufacturers of the Packard and acquired what they wanted elsewhere. The manufacturers of the Packard did not record massive profits! The most useful products from the point of view of consumers turn out to be the most profitable. Were I to turn my clumsy hands to the making of clay models of Miss Piggy, I fear few admirers of that gracious lady would purchase my product. They want a model which looks like Miss Piggy! The needs of people dictate who does, and who does not, make a "profit."

The Customer's Choice

Yet the matter is more significant than that. Once upon a time people getting rid of their garbage either threw it into a garbage can or wrapped it in newspaper and put the resulting parcel into the garbage can. Then someone, somewhere, thought of plastic bags which, lining a garbage can, would make life easier and garbage cans less smelly! *What was the first question that person had to ask?* He had to ask what people would be prepared to pay for such bags! Would they pay $10? No—people would prefer either to keep that $10 or procure two paperback novels than to surrender that $10 or forgo two paperback novels and own a plastic bag for the disposal of garbage. Would they pay $1? Maybe—but most people would prefer to forgo the possession of the bag and procure, say, a pack of cigarettes than to forgo the pack of cigarettes and obtain the bag. Would they pay 30¢? That sounds reasonable. Now what does the maker of plastic garbage disposable bags have to do? (He could, of course, reject the free market and try to charm a politician into making the purchase and use of such bags compulsory, but that is to reject both the free society and the market. Let us, however, ignore this cheat!) What he must do is find a way of manufacturing such bags *below* the "price" set by consumers. If he works out a way to make such bags for 1¢ he stands to make a "high" profit. Sadly—at least for the manufacturer—such a high profit would signal to others that they should get into the act and reduce the price of such bags—and make more modest, yet tolerable, profits! The critical point, however, is that profits demonstrate that producers have found ways whereby they use resources to produce a product at costs *below* the value people place upon the product. *Profits are residuals.* They represent not something wickedly "added" to a price, but the difference between a people-determined price and the costs of manufacturing some commodity.

Yet again, that is but part of the story. The time, physical labor, and resources which go into the making of plastic garbage bags *could* have been used to create some other commodity. How does one work out whether to use these resources to produce garbage bags, or some other product? *The answer lies in the magic word "profit."* For profits simply show that people *want* disposable plastic garbage bags more than they want, say, plastic slippers! The company making large profits—in a genuinely free market—is using material resources, time, labor, and intelligence in a way satisfying what people want and need rather than using the same "ingredients" in ways which do *not* satisfy what people want and need. Limited resources are being allocated in a people-serving, responsible way.

No Apology Needed

To "apologize" for profits is to put on the heavy armor of Saul. Defenders of the philosophy of liberty *do* have a Goliath of prejudice and error to fight when it comes to "profits," but they must not weigh themselves down by carrying an unnecessary load. Carefully, cogently, and non-aggressively, they must explain what profits are and why they are not "evil." There is no other way.

David won. The mighty Goliath, sheathed in his bronze armor, was defeated by a youth bearing five stones, a shepherd's bag, and a conviction that he came to do battle in the name of the "Lord of hosts."

Truth is mighty, and it *will* prevail. The battle is not easy, but in truth the socialists have already lost. Their many experiments have failed. Yet their voice, like that of Goliath, resonates like thunder and brings terror to the hearts of many. There is a fight to be fought, and the defender of liberty faces difficult tasks. Hence, such a defender must say "No!" to the armor of Saul. He must not wear what weighs him down. He must not carry burdens that in truth are not his to carry. His advisers, like King Saul, "mean well." But like the lithesome youth, he must be careful.

"Saul made David put on his own armor and put a bronze helmet on his head and gave him his own breast plate to wear, and over David's armor he buckled his own sword; but . . . David found he could not walk. 'I cannot walk with these,' he said to Saul . . . So they took them off."[7]

---

1. J. Pavlevski, "Economies et Sociétés," *Journal of the Institute of the Applied Sciences*, Geneva, February 1969.
2. J. F. Revel, "The View from Paris," *Encounter*, December 1980.
3. Ludwig von Mises, *Bureaucracy* (Grove City, Pa.: Libertarian Press, 1989).
4. Adam Smith, *The Wealth of Nations* (Indianapolis, Ind.: Liberty Press, 1981), p. 145.
5. A. N. Whitehead *et al.*, *Principia Mathematica* (New York: Cambridge University Press, 1910–13), three volumes.
6. Ludwig von Mises, *Human Action* (Chicago: Henry Regnery Company, 1968), third revised edition.
7. Samuel, chapter 17, verses 38–39.

Economics for the Teachable

by Leonard E. Read

The teachable—those who aspire to an ever greater understanding—are those with an awareness of how little they know.[1] Lest teachableness and lowliness or inferiority be associated, consider the case for teachableness and wisdom as having a relationship.

Said Socrates, "This man thinks he knows something when he does not, whereas I, as I do not know anything, do not think I do, either." For such acknowledgments of fallibility, Socrates was acclaimed a wise man. He and many others—for instance, Lecomte du Nouy and Robert Milliken, scientists of our time—discovered, as they expanded their own consciousness, that they progressively exposed themselves to more and more of the unknown. Edison's fact-packed, inquiring, ever-curious mind concluded that, "We don't know a millionth of one per cent about anything. We are just emerging from the chimpanzee state." These teachable persons came to realize how little they knew and that, perhaps, is a measure of wisdom.

For the student of economics, this poses an interesting question: Is it possible to have a workable, productive economy premised on a society of teachable individuals, those who are aware that they know very little?

We can assume that such an economy would differ markedly from the planned society of egotists or know-it-alls, those at the other end of the intellectual spectrum, the ones who see no difficulties at all in arranging the lives of everyone else in accord with their designs. Further, they are quite willing to resort to the police force to implement their schemes for improving society by nationalizing it.

A group of seven economists, for example, recently voiced this view: "The federal government is our only instrument for guiding the economic destiny of the country."[2]

Mr. Read (1898–1983) founded FEE in 1946. A visionary and inspirational leader, he was FEE's president until his death. A prolific writer, he excelled at puncturing intellectual bombast and elucidating timeless principles in clear, everyday language. This article originally appeared in the January 1960 issue of *The Freeman*.

Some of the Problems

Government, in such a role, must be staffed largely with those who are unaware of how little they know, who have no qualms about their ability to plan and regulate the national economic growth, set wages, prescribe hours of work, write the price tags for everything, decide how much of what shall be produced or grown, expand or contract the money supply arbitrarily, set interest rates and rents, subsidize with other peoples' earnings whatever activity strikes their fancy, lend billions in money not voluntarily entrusted to them, allocate the fruits of the labor of all to foreign governments of their choice—in short, decide what shall be taken from each Peter and how much of the "take" shall be paid to each Paul.

Government control and ownership of the means of production is socialism, sometimes called "state interventionism" or "communism," depending on the degree of disparagement intended. It rests on the premise that certain persons possess the intelligence to understand and guide all human action. Socialism or state interventionism is advocated by those who sense no lack of this prescience in themselves, by the naive followers of such claimants, by the seekers of power over others, by those who foresee an advantage to themselves in such manipulations, and by the "do-gooders" who fail to distinguish between police grants-in-aid and the Judeo-Christian principles of charity. All in all, they are a considerable number, but still a minority of the tens of millions whose lives they would regulate.

The most important point to bear in mind is that socialism presupposes that government or officialdom is the endower, dispenser, and the source of men's rights, as well as the guide, controller, and director of their energies. This is the Supremacy of Egotism: The State is God; we are the State!

Let us then examine the competency of a typical egotist. It matters not whom you choose—a professor, a professional politician, a Napoleon, a Hitler, a Stalin—but the more pretentious the better.[3] Simply admit some supreme egotist into your mind's eye and take stock of him. Study his private life. You will usually discover that his wife, his children, his neighbors, those in his hire, fail to respond to his dictates in ways he thinks proper.[4] This is to say, the egotist is frequently a failure in the very situations nearest and best known to him. Incongruously, he then concludes that he is called to manage whole societies—or even the world! Fie on anything small enough to occupy an ordinary man!

The Planner's Incompetence

Let's further test the knowledge of the egotist. He wants to plan production; what does he know about it? For example, there is a company in the United States which manufactures well over 200,000 separate items. No one person in the company knows what these items are and there is no individual on the face of the earth who has the skills, by himself, to make any one of them.[5] It's a safe bet that the egotist under examination has never been closer to this company than a textbook description by some fellow egotists. Yet, he would put this intricate, voluntary mechanism under the rigid control of government and would have no hesitancy at all in accepting the post of Chief Administrator. He would then arbitrarily allocate and price all raw materials and manpower and, after long and complicated statistics of the past, arbitarily allocate and price the more than 200,000 items, most of which he never knew existed. Involved in the operations of this company alone—a mere fraction of the American economy—are incalculable human energy exchanges, many billions of them annually; but the egotist would manage these with a few "big man" gestures! Such cursory attention he would find necessary for, bear in mind, he also would have under his control the lives, livelihoods, and activities of the millions of individuals not directly associated with this company.

Next, what does the egotist know about exchange? In a specialized or division-of-labor economy like ours, exchange cannot be carried on by primitive barter. It is accomplished by countless interchanges interacting on one another with the aid of a generally accepted medium of exchange or money. The socialistic philosophy of the egotists presupposes that there are persons competent to regulate and control the volume and value of money and credit. Yet, surely no one person or committee is any more competent to manipulate the supply of money and credit to attain a definite end than he or a committee is able to make an automobile or a wooden lead pencil!

An economy founded on the premise of know-it-allness is patently absurd.

But, can there be a sensible, rational economy founded on the premise of know-next-to-nothingness? An economy that would run rings around socialism? In short, is there a highly productive way of life which presupposes no human prescience, no infallibility, nothing beyond an awareness that it is not the role of man to pattern others in his own image? *There is such a way!*

The Creator as Sovereign

Contrary to socialism, this way of life for teachable people, who concede their fallibility, denies that government, staffed by fallible people, is the source of men's rights. It holds, instead, that men "are endowed by their Creator with certain unalienable rights, that among these are Life, Liberty, and the pursuit of Happiness. That to secure these rights, governments are instituted among men. . . ." With this as a premise, sovereignty—the source of rights—rests with the Creator; government is but a man-made means to protect this arrangement between man and his Creator. When Creativity is assumed to exist over and beyond the conscious mind of man, a whole new concept of man's relationship to man emerges. Man, once he conceives of himself in this setting, knows that he is not knowledgeable but, at best, is only teachable. The greatest conscious fact of his life is his awareness of the Unknown.

To illustrate, let us observe how such a person "builds" his own house. He does not think of himself as actually having built it. No man living could do that. He thinks of himself as having done only an assembly job. He is aware of numerous preconditions, two of which are:

1. The provision of his materials. Others cut trees, sawed them into boards which were kiln dried, planed, grooved, held in waiting, delivered. Some mined ore, assembled blast furnaces from which came the metals for saws, planes, pipes, tubs, nails, hardware. There were those who assembled the machinery to mine the ore and those who assembled the machine tools to make the machinery. There were those who saved the fruits of their labor and loaned or invested it that there might be these tools. There were

the growers of flax and soybeans, the extractors of their oils, chemists, paint makers. Others wrote books about mixing concrete, architecture, engineering, construction. There were publishers, typesetters—how does one make a linotype machine?—on and on, creative energies and energy exchanges through time and space, ad infinitum!

2. A reasonable absence of destructive energies. No thieves stole his supplies. Those who supplied him had not defrauded him nor had they misrepresented their wares. Violence, like coercively keeping men from working where they chose (strikes) or like coercively keeping men from freely exchanging the products of their labor (protectionism) had not succeeded in denying these services to him. In short, interferences with creative efforts and exchanges had not reached the point where a house was impossible.

The man who knows how little he knows is aware that creative energies, and creative energy exchanges, work miracles if unhampered. The evidence is all about him. There is his automobile, the coffee he drinks, the meat he eats, the clothes he wears, the symphony he hears, the books he reads, the painting he sees, the perfume he smells, the velvet he touches and, above all, the insights or inspiration or ideas that come to him—from where he does not know.

Respect for the Unknown

The teachable person looks with awe upon all creation.[6] He agrees that "only God can make a tree." And he also understands that, in the final analysis, only God can build a house. Nature, Creation, God—use your own term—if not interfered with, will combine atoms into molecules which then configurated in one manner will form a tree, in another manner a blade of grass, in still another manner a rose—mysteries upon mysteries! And, there are demonstrations all around him that the creative energies of men, when not interfered with, do, through space and time, configurate, in response to human necessity and aspiration, to form houses, symphonies, foods, clothes, airplanes—things in endless profusion.

The teachable person is likely to be aware of some wonderful cosmic force at work—a drawing, attracting, magnetic power—attending to perpetual creation. He may well conceive of himself as an agent through whom this power has the potentiality of flowing and, to the extent this occurs, to that degree does he have an opportunity to share in the processes of creation. As agent, his psychological problem is to rid himself of his own inhibitory influences—fear, superstition, anger, and the like—in order that this power may freely flow. He knows that he cannot dictate to it, direct it, or even get results by commanding, "Now I shall be inspired" or "Now I shall create a symphony" or "Now I shall discover a cure for the common cold" or "Now I shall invent a way of impressing upon others how little they know." He is quite certain he must not thwart this power as it pertains to his own personal being.

Society-wise, the teachable human being, the one who conceives of himself as agent through whom this mysterious, creative power has the potentiality of flowing, concedes that what applies to him must, perforce, apply to other human beings; that this same power has the potentiality of flowing through them; that his existence, his livelihood, his own opportunity to serve as an agency of the power, *depends* on how well these others fare creatively. He realizes that he can no more dictate its flow in others than in himself. He knows only that he must not thwart it in others and that it is to his interest and theirs, and to the interest of all society, that there be no thwarting of this force in others by anyone. Leave this power alone and let it work its miracles!

Thwarting Creative Action

Creative action cannot be induced by any form of authoritarianism, be the commands directed at oneself or at others. However, any idiot can thwart these actions in himself or in others, precisely as he can thwart the forces of creation from manifesting themselves as a tree. He can prevent a tree from being, but he can't make it be. Coercive force can only inhibit, restrain, penalize, destroy. It cannot create!

The teachable individual imposes no inhibitions, restraints, or penalties on creative actions. He leaves them free to pursue their miraculous courses.

The man who knows how little he knows would like to see the removal of all destructive obstacles to the flow of creative energy and energy exchanges. But even this he doesn't quite know how to accomplish. He would rely mostly on an improved understanding of the Golden Rule, the Ten Commandments, and other consistent ethical and moral principles. He hopes that more and more persons eventually will see that even their own self-interest is never served by impairing the creative actions of others, or living off them as parasites.

Government's Limited Role

In summary, then, the teachable person is content to leave creative energies and their exchanges untouched; and he would rely primarily on ethical precepts and practices to keep these energy circuits free of destructive invasion. The governmental apparatus would merely assist these precepts and practices by defending the life and property of all citizens equally; by protecting all willing exchange and restraining all unwilling exchange; by suppressing and penalizing all fraud, all misrepresentation, all violence, all predatory practices; by invoking a common justice under written law; and by keeping the records incidental thereto.

Very well. So far, in theory, creative energies or actions and their exchanges are left unhampered. Destructive actions are self-disciplined or, if not, are restrained by the societal agency of law and defensive force. Is that all? Does not the person who is aware of how little he knows have to know a lot of economics?

Why Pay for Things?

The man, mentioned previously, who "built" his own house, has about as much economic understanding as is necessary. He reflects on all the countless antecedent services which he assembled into a finished home. Originally, all of these items came from Nature. They were there when the Indians foraged this same territory. There was no price on them in their raw state—they were for free, so to speak. Yet, he paid—let us say—$10,000 for them.

What was the payment for? Well, when we slice through all the economic terms, he paid for the human action that necessarily had to be applied to things of the good earth. He paid for actions and energies which he himself did not possess, or possessing, did not choose to exert. Were he limited to his own energies to bring about the services antecedent to his assembly of them, he could not have built such a home in a thousand lifetimes.

These human actions for which he paid took several forms. Generalizing, his $10,000 covered salaries and wages that had been paid for judgment, foresight, skill, initiative, enterprise, research, management, invention, physical exertion, chance discovery, know-how; interest that had been paid for self-denial or waiting; dividends that had been paid for risking; rent that had been paid for locational advantage—in short, all of the $10,000 covered payments for one or another form of human action. Literally millions of individuals had a hand in the process.

Let the Market Decide

The major economic problem—the root of economic hassles—reduced to its simplest terms, revolves around the question of who is going to get how much of that $10,000. How is economic justice to be determined?What part shall go to the grower of soybeans, to the investor in a saw mill, to the man who tends the machine that pours nails into wooden kegs, to the inventor of the machine, to the owner of the paint plant? *Who shall determine the answers?*

How much economics does one have to know to settle, in one's own mind, how and by whom economic justice shall be rendered? He has to know only this: *Let the payment for each individual's contribution be determined by what others will offer in willing exchange.* That's all there is to an economy for those who know they know not. It is that simple.[7]

The concept underlying such an economy—never formalized until the year 1871—is known as the marginal utility theory of value. It also goes by two other names: "the subjective theory of value" and "the free market theory of value." Testimony to its simplicity was given by Eugen von Böhm-Bawerk, one of its greatest theoreticians:

> And so the intellectual labor that people have to perform in estimating subjective value is not so astounding as may appear . . . incidentally, even if it were a considerably greater task than it actually is, one could still confidently entrust it to "John Doe and Richard Roe." . . . For centuries, long before science set up the doctrine of marginal utility, the common man was accustomed to seek things and abandon things . . . he practiced the doctrine of marginal utility before economic theory discovered it.[8]

The labor theory of value held scholarly sway prior to this free market theory. It contended that value was determined by the amount of effort expended or fatigue incurred. For example, some persons made mud pies, others, mince pies. The same effort, let us assume, is expended in the preparation of each. Under the labor theory of value the mud pie makers should receive the same return for their efforts as the mince pie makers. The only way to accomplish this—consumers being unwilling to exchange the fruits of their labor for mud pies—is for the government to subsidize the mud pie makers by taking from the mince pie makers. Karl Marx elaborated upon and helped systematize this theory—governments taking from the productive and subsidizing the less productive.

The labor theory of value, proved over and over again to be the enemy of both justice and sound economics, nonetheless, continues to gain in popular acceptance. Emotional reactions to effort expended and fatigue incurred do not readily give way to reason. Sentimental thoughts, such as "the poor, hard-working farmers," set the political stage for agricultural subsidies. Similarly, sympathies which emanate from such outmoded and erroneous reflections as "the down-trodden laboring man" condition most people to accept the coercive powers allowed labor unions.

Practice of the labor theory of value is rationalized by spenders, inflationists, Keynesians, egotists, on the ground that it puts purchasing power in the hands of those who will spend it. As set forth earlier, this man-concocted system of forcibly controlling creative human action—interventionism, socialism, communism—presupposes all-knowing bureaucrats but, to date, not a single one has been found, not even a reasonable facsimile.

The free market, on the other hand, is for the teachable, who know their own limitations, who feel no compulsions to play God, and who put their faith in voluntary, willing exchange—a manner of human relationships that miraculously works economic wonders for all without requiring infallibility of anyone.

---

1. *The teachable shall inherit the earth* appears to be a sensible interpretation of the Biblical pronouncement, "The meek shall inherit the earth." It is quite obvious that "the meek" had no reference to the Mr. Milquetoasts in society.

2. See *First National City Bank Letter* for August 1959, p. 90.

3. "A high-brow is a low-brow plus pretentiousness," said H. G. Wells.

4. Napoleon's domestic affairs were a mess and his numerous family drove him to distraction; Hitler was an indifferent paper hanger; Stalin tried first theology and then train

robbery before he elected bureaucracy and dictatorship; many bureaucrats charged with great affairs have no record of personal success.

5. See my "I, Pencil" for a demonstration that no one person knows how to make an item even as simple as a wooden lead pencil.

6. "If I may coin a new English word to translate a much nicer old Greek word, 'wanting-to-know-it-ness' was their characteristic; wonder . . . was the mother of their philosophy." *The Challenge of the Greek* by T. R. Glover (New York: The Macmillan Company, 1942), pp. 6–7.

7. There are some who will contend that one must understand money, the medium of exchange. This, also, is an impossible requirement. For extended comments on this point of view, see my *Government: An Ideal Concept* (Irvington-on-Hudson, N.Y.: Foundation for Economic Education, Inc., 1954), pp. 80–91.

8. Eugen von Böhm-Bawerk, *Capital and Interest* (South Holland, Ill.: Libertarian Press, 1959), Vol. II, pp. 203–204.

II. THE JUDEO-CHRISTIAN TRADITION

The Moral Element in Free Enterprise

by F. A. Hayek

Economic activity provides the material means for all our ends. At the same time, most of our individual efforts are directed to providing means for the ends of others in order that they, in turn, may provide us with the means for our ends. It is only because we are free in the choice of our means that we are also free in the choice of our ends.

Economic freedom is thus an indispensable condition of all other freedom, and free enterprise both a necessary condition and a consequence of personal freedom. In discussing The Moral Element in Free Enterprise I shall therefore not confine myself to the problems of economic life but consider the general relations between freedom and morals.

By freedom in this connection I mean, in the great Anglo-Saxon tradition, independence of the arbitrary will of another. This is the classical conception of freedom under the law, a state of affairs in which a man may be coerced only where coercion is required by the general rules of law, equally applicable to all, and never by the discretionary decision of administrative authority.

The relationship between this freedom and moral values is mutual and complex. I shall therefore have to confine myself to bringing out the salient points in something like telegraphic style.

It is, on the one hand, an old discovery that morals and moral values will grow only in an environment of freedom, and that, in general, moral standards of people and classes are high only where they have long enjoyed freedom—and proportional to the amount of freedom they have possessed. It is also an old insight that a free society will work well only where free action is guided by strong moral beliefs, and, therefore, that we shall enjoy all the benefits of freedom only where freedom is already well established. To this I want to add that freedom, if it is to work well, requires not only

Dr. F. A. Hayek (1899–1992), a disciple of Ludwig von Mises, and one of the seminal thinkers of the 20th century, was the author of such classics as *The Road to Serfdom* and *The Constitution of Liberty*. He won the Nobel Prize for Economics in 1974. This article originally appeared in the July 1962 issue of *The Freeman*.

strong moral standards but moral standards of a particular kind, and that it is possible in a free society for moral standards to grow up which, if they become general, will destroy freedom and with it the basis of all moral values.

Forgotten Truths

Before I turn to this point, which is not generally understood, I must briefly elaborate upon the two old truths which ought to be familiar but which are often forgotten. That freedom is the matrix required for the growth of moral values—indeed not merely one value among many but the source of all values—is almost self-evident. It is only where the individual has choice, and its inherent responsibility, that he has occasion to affirm existing values, to contribute to their further growth, and to earn moral merit. Obedience has moral value only where it is a matter of choice and not of coercion. It is in the order in which we rank our different ends that our moral sense manifests itself; and in applying the general rules of morals to particular situations each individual is constantly called upon to interpret and apply the general principles and in doing so to create particular values.

I have no time here for showing how this has in fact brought it about that free societies not only have generally been law-abiding societies, but also in modern times have been the source of all the great humanitarian movements aiming at active help to the weak, the ill, and the oppressed. Unfree societies, on the other hand, have as regularly developed a disrespect for the law, a callous attitude to suffering, and even sympathy for the malefactor.

I must turn to the other side of the medal. It should also be obvious that the results of freedom must depend on the values which free individuals pursue. It would be impossible to assert that a free society will always and necessarily develop values of which we would approve, or even, as we shall see, that it will maintain values which are compatible with the preservation of freedom. All that we can say is that the values we hold are the product of freedom, that in particular the Christian values had to assert themselves through men who successfully resisted coercion by government, and that it is to the desire to be able to follow one's own moral convictions that we owe the modern safeguards of individual freedom. Perhaps we can add to this that only societies which hold moral values essentially similar to our own have survived as free societies, while in others freedom has perished.

All this provides strong argument why it is most important that a free society be based on strong moral convictions and why if we want to preserve freedom *and* morals, we should do all in our power to spread the appropriate moral convictions. But what I am mainly concerned with is the error that men must first be good before they can be granted freedom.

It is true that a free society lacking a moral foundation would be a very unpleasant society in which to live. But it would even so be better than a society which is unfree and immoral; and it at least offers the hope of a gradual emergence of moral convictions which an unfree society prevents. On this point I am afraid I strongly disagree with John Stuart Mill, who maintained that until men have attained the capacity of being guided to their own improvement by conviction or persuasion, "there is nothing for them but implicit obedience to an Akbar or Charlemagne, if they are so fortunate as to find one." Here I believe T. B. Macaulay expressed the much greater wisdom of an older tradition when he wrote that "many politicians of our time are in the habit of laying it down as a self-evident proposition that no people are to be free till they are fit to use their freedom. The maxim is worthy of the fool in the old story, who resolved not to go into the water till he had learned to swim. If men are to wait for liberty till they become wise and good, they may indeed wait forever."

Moral Considerations

But I must now turn from what is merely the reaffirmation of old wisdom to more critical issues. I have said that liberty, to work well, requires not merely the existence of strong moral convictions but also the acceptance of particular moral views. By this I do *not* mean that within limits utilitarian considerations will contribute to alter moral views on particular issues. Nor do I mean that, as Edwin Cannan expressed it, "of the two principles, Equity and Economy, Equity is ultimately the weaker . . . the judgment of mankind about what is equitable is liable to change, and . . . one of the forces that causes it to change is mankind's discovery from time to time that what was supposed to be quite just and equitable in some particular matter has become, or perhaps always was, uneconomical."

This is also true and important, though it may not be a commendation to all people. I am concerned rather with some more general conceptions which seem to me an essential condition of a free society and without which it cannot survive. The two crucial ones seem to me the belief in individual responsibility and the approval as just of an arrangement by which material rewards are made to correspond to the value which a person's particular services have to his fellow; *not* to the esteem in which he is held as a whole person for his moral merit.

Responsible Individuals

I must be brief on the first point—which I find very difficult. Modern developments here are part of the story of the destruction of moral value by scientific error which has recently been my chief concern—and what a scholar happens to be working on at the moment tends to appear to him as the most important subject in the world. But I shall try to say what belongs here in a very few words.

Free societies have always been societies in which the belief in individual responsibility has been strong. They have allowed individuals to act on *their* knowledge and beliefs and have treated the results achieved as due to them. The aim was to make it worthwhile for people to act rationally and reasonably and to persuade them that what they would achieve depended chiefly on them. This last belief is undoubtedly not entirely correct, but it certainly had a wonderful effect in developing both initiative and circumspection.

By a curious confusion it has come to be thought that this belief in individual responsibility has been refuted by growing insight into the manner in which events generally, and human actions in particular, are determined by certain classes of causes. It is probably true that we have gained increasing understanding of the *kinds* of circumstances which affect human action—but no more. We can certainly not say that a particular conscious act of any man is the necessary result of particular circumstances that we can specify—leaving out his peculiar individuality built up by the whole of his history. Of our generic knowledge as to how human action can be influenced we make use in assessing praise and blame—which we do for the purpose of making people behave in a desirable fashion. It is on this limited determinism—as much as our knowledge in fact justifies—that the belief in responsibility is based, while only a belief in some metaphysical self which stands outside the chain of cause and effect could justify the contention that it is useless to hold the individual responsible for his actions.

The Pressure of Opinion

Yet, crude as is the fallacy underlying the opposite and supposedly scientific view, it has had the most profound effect in destroying the chief device which society has developed to assure decent conduct—the pressure of opinion making people observe the rules of the game. And it has ended in that *Myth of Mental Illness* which a distinguished psychiatrist, Dr. T. S. Szasz, has recently justly castigated in a book so titled. We have probably not yet discovered the best way of teaching people to live according to rules which make life in society for them and their fellows not too unpleasant. But in our present state of knowledge I am sure that we shall never build up a successful free society without that pressure of praise and blame which treats the individual as responsible for his conduct and also makes him bear the consequences of even innocent error.

But if it is essential for a free society that the esteem in which a person is held by his fellows depends on how far he lives up to the demand for moral law, it is also essential that material reward should *not* be determined by the opinion of his fellows of his moral merits but by the value which they attach to the particular services he renders them. This brings me to my second chief point: the conception of social justice which must prevail if a free society is to be preserved. This is the point on which the defenders of a free society and the advocates of a collectivist system are chiefly divided. And on this point, while the advocates of the socialist conception of distributive justice are usually very outspoken, the upholders of freedom are unnecessarily shy about stating bluntly the implications of their ideal.

Why Liberty?

The simple facts are these: We want the individual to have liberty because only if *he* can decide what to do can he also use all his unique combination of information, skills, and capacities which nobody else can fully appreciate. To enable the individual to fulfill his potential we must also allow him to act on his own estimates of the various chances and probabilities. Since we do not know what he knows, we cannot decide whether his decisions were justified; nor can we know whether his success or failure was due to his efforts and foresight, or to good luck. In other words, we must look at results, not intentions or motives, and can allow him to act on his own knowledge only if we also allow him to keep what his fellows are willing to pay him for his services, irrespective of whether we think this reward appropriate to the moral merit he has earned or the esteem in which we hold him as a person.

Such remuneration, in accordance with the value of a man's services, inevitably is often very different from what we think of his moral merit. This, I believe, is the chief source of the dissatisfaction with a free enterprise system and of the clamor for "distributive justice." It is neither honest nor effective to deny that there is such a discrepancy between the moral merit and esteem which a person may earn by his actions and, on the other hand, the value of the services for which we pay him. We place ourselves in an entirely false position if we try to gloss over this fact or to disguise it. Nor have we any need to do so.

Material Rewards

It seems to me one of the great merits of a free society that material reward is *not* dependent on whether the majority of our fellows like or esteem us personally. This means that, so long as we keep within the accepted rules, moral pressure can be brought on us only through the esteem of those whom we ourselves respect and not through the allocation of material reward by a social authority. It is of the essence of a free society that we should be materially rewarded not for doing what others order us to do, but for giving them what they want. Our conduct ought certainly to be guided by our desire for their esteem. But we are free because the success of our daily efforts does not depend on whether particular people like us, or our principles, or our religion, or our manners, and because *we* can decide whether the material reward others are prepared to pay for our services makes it worthwhile for us to render them.

We seldom know whether a brilliant idea which a man suddenly conceives, and which may greatly benefit his fellows, is the result of years of effort and preparatory investment, or whether it is a sudden inspiration induced by an accidental combination of knowledge and circumstance. But we do know that, where in a given instance it has been the former, it would not have been worthwhile to take the risk if the discoverer were not allowed to reap the benefit. And since we do not know how to distinguish one case from the other, we must also allow a man to get the gain when his good fortune is a matter of luck.

The Moral Merit of a Person

I do not wish to deny, I rather wish to emphasize, that in our society personal esteem and material success are much too closely bound together. We ought to be much more aware that if we regard a man as entitled to a high material reward that in itself does not necessarily entitle him to high esteem. And, though we are often confused on this point, it does not mean that his confusion is a necessary result of the free enterprise system—or that in general the free enterprise system is more materialistic than other social orders. Indeed, and this brings me to the last point I want to make, it seems to me in many respects considerably less so.

In fact free enterprise has developed the only kind of society which, while it provides us with ample material means, if that is what we mainly want, still leaves the individual free to choose between material and nonmaterial reward. The confusion of which I have been speaking—between the value which a man's services have to his fellows and the esteem he deserves for his moral merit—*may* well make a free enterprise society materialistic. But the way to prevent this is certainly not to place the control of all material means under a single direction, to make the distribution of material goods the chief concern of all common effort, and thus to get politics and economics inextricably mixed.

Many Bases for Judging

It is at least possible for a free enterprise society to be in this respect a pluralistic society which knows no single order of rank but has many different principles on which esteem is based; where worldly success is neither the only evidence nor regarded as certain proof of individual merit. It may well be true that periods of a very rapid increase of wealth, in which many enjoy the benefits of wealth for the first time, tend to produce for a time a predominant concern with material improvement. Until the recent European upsurge many members of the more comfortable classes there used to decry as materialistic the economically more active periods to which they owed the material comfort which had made it easy for them to devote themselves to other things.

Cultural Progress Follows

Periods of great cultural and artistic creativity have generally followed, rather than coincided with, the periods of the most rapid increase in wealth. To my mind this shows *not* that a free society must be dominated by material concerns but rather that with freedom it is the moral atmosphere in the widest sense, the values which people hold, which will determine the chief direction of their activities. Individuals as well as communities, when they feel that other things have become more important than material advance, can turn to them. It is certainly not by the endeavor to make material reward correspond to all merit, but only by frankly recognizing that there are other and often more important goals than material success, that we can guard ourselves against becoming too materialistic.

Surely it is unjust to blame a system as more materialistic because it leaves it to the individual to decide whether he prefers material gain to other kinds of excellence, instead of having this decided for him. There is indeed little merit in being idealistic if the provision of the material means required for these idealistic aims is left to somebody else. It is only where a person can himself choose to make a material sacrifice for a nonmaterial end that he deserves credit. The desire to be relieved of the choice, and of any need for personal sacrifice, certainly does not seem to me particularly idealistic.

I must say that I find the atmosphere of the advanced Welfare State in every sense more materialistic than that of a free enterprise society. If the latter gives individuals much more scope to serve their fellows by the pursuit of purely materialistic aims, it also gives them the opportunity to pursue any other aim they regard as more important. One must remember, however, that the pure idealism of an aim is questionable whenever the material means necessary for its fulfillment have been created by others.

Means and Ends

In conclusion, I want for a moment to return to the point from which I started. When we defend the free enterprise system we must always remember that it deals only with means. What we make of our freedom is up to us. We must not confuse efficiency in providing means with the purposes which they serve. A society which has no other standard than efficiency will indeed waste that efficiency. If men are to be free to use their talents to provide us with the means we want, we must remunerate them in accordance with the value these means have to us. Nevertheless, we ought to esteem them only in accordance with the use they make of the means at *their* disposal.

Let us encourage usefulness to one's fellows by all means, but let us not confuse it with the importance of the ends which men ultimately serve. It is the glory of the free enterprise system that it makes it at least possible that each individual, while serving his fellows, can do so for his own ends. But the system is itself only a means, and its infinite possibilities must be used in the service of ends which exist apart.

Think Twice Before You Disparage Capitalism

by Perry E. Gresham

"Everybody for himself," said the elephant as he danced around among the chickens. This lampoon of capitalism came from a Canadian politician. The word "capitalism" has fallen into disrepute. It is associated with other pejorative terms such as "fat cat," "big business," "military-industrial complex," "greedy industrialists," "standpatters," "reactionaries," and "property values without regard to human values." Many serious scholars look on capitalism as a transitional system between late feudalism and inevitable socialism.

Adam Smith has been associated with the word "capitalism" even though he did not use the term. He did not so much as refer to capital by that name, but used the word "stock" to describe what we call capital. Karl Marx wrote in response to Adam Smith's *Wealth of Nations* and called his great work *Das Kapital.* There was disparagement and scorn—even hate—for the ideas of the free market economy. The term capitalism has been less than appealing to many people since that time even though they know little about the contents of the Marx benchmark in political economy.

Some political economists who cherish individual liberty and the free market have suggested that a new name be found to describe economic liberty and individual responsibility. Until a new name appears, however, the thoughtful person does well to think twice before he disparages the market economy with all of its implications implied by the term capitalism since there is now no ready alternative available for reasonable discourse.

Is the System Outmoded?

Many thoughtful citizens of America think of capitalism as a quaint and vanishing vestige of our Yankee industrial beginnings.

Dr. Perry E. Gresham (1907–1994) was for many years president of Bethany College in West Virginia, and served for a year as acting president of FEE. This article originally appeared in the March 1977 issue of *The Freeman.*

With burgeoning population, urbanization and industrialization, they argue, capitalism disappears. They are not quite ready to embrace socialism, but they heartily approve government planning and intervention. John Kenneth Galbraith, articulate spokesman for the liberal establishment, calls for the open acclaim of a new socialism which he believes to be both imminent and necessary. "The new socialism allows of no acceptable alternatives; it cannot be escaped except at the price of grave discomfort, considerable social disorder and, on occasion, lethal damage to health and well-being. The new socialism is not ideological; it is compelled by circumstance."[1]

At first blush, the Marxian assumption of economic determinism is quite plausible, but I do not believe it can stand up to the scrutiny of experience. My study of history leads me to assume with many of my thoughtful colleagues that free people can, within certain limits, choose their own systems of political economy. This is precisely what happened in West Germany at the time of Ludwig Erhard. The Germans chose capitalism rather than the socialism recommended by many American, British, and Continental economists and politicians. It is my opinion that Americans can and should call for a renewal of capitalism rather than a new socialism.

Capitalism has been neither understood nor sympathetically considered by most contemporary Americans. Capitalism is a radical and appealing system of political economy which needs a new and favorable review. The new socialism has never been tried. The old socialism is not very inviting. Consider Russia, China, Cuba, Chile, and now [i.e., 1977] Britain. Capitalism has been tried with the most amazing success in all history. What is the nature of a political and economic system which has made the poor people of America more prosperous than the rich of many countries operating under State control? Here are my paragraphs in praise of capitalism. They are somewhat lyrical but grounded in fact and open to review.

An Enviable Record

Capitalism is the one system of political economy which works, has worked and, given a chance, will continue to work. The alternative system is socialism. Socialism is seductive in theory, but tends toward tyranny and serfdom in practice.

Capitalism was not born with *The Wealth of Nations,* nor will it die with *Das Kapital.* It is as old as history and as new as a paper route for a small boy. Capitalism is a point of view and a way of life. Its principles apply whether or not they are understood, approved, and cherished.

Capitalism is no relic of Colonial America. It has the genius of freedom to change with the times and to meet the challenges of big industries, big unions, and big government if it can free itself from the restraints of interest-group intervention which eventuates in needless government expansion and spending. Let the market work, and the ambition of each individual will serve the common good of society.

Capitalism is an economic system which believes with Locke and Jefferson that life, liberty, and property are among the inalienable rights of man.

Capitalism denies the banal dichotomy between property values and human values. Property values *are* human values. Imagine the disjunction when it is applied to a person with a mechanical limb or a cardiac pacemaker. The workman with his tools and the farmer with his land are almost as dramatic in the exemplification of the identity between a person and his property.

Capitalism is belief in man—an assumption that prosperity and happiness are best achieved when each person lives by his own will and his own intelligence. Each person is a responsible citizen.

Limited Government

Capitalism recognizes the potential tyranny of any government. The government is made for man, not man for the government. Therefore, government should be limited in size and function, lest free individuals lose their identity and become wards of the State. Frederic Bastiat has called the State a "great fiction wherein everybody tries to live at the expense of everybody else."

Capitalism denies the naive and mystic faith in the State to control wages and prices. A fair price is the amount agreed upon by the buyer and seller. Competition in a free market is far more trustworthy than any government administrator. The government is a worthy defense against force and fraud, but the market is much better at protecting against monopoly, inflation, soaring prices, depressed wages and the problems of scarcity. Capitalism works to the advantage of consumer and worker alike.

Capitalism denies the right of government to take the property of a private citizen at will, or to tax away his livelihood at will, or to tell him when and where he must work or how and where he must live. Capitalism is built on the firm foundation of individual liberty.

Capitalism believes that every person deserves an opportunity. "All men are created equal" in terms of opportunity, but people are not equal—nor should they be. How dull a world in which nobody could outrun anybody! Competition is a good thing no matter how much people try to avoid it. Equality and liberty are contradictory. Capitalism chooses liberty!

Equality of Opportunity

Capitalism gives a poor person an opportunity to become rich. It does not lock people into the condition of poverty. It calls on every individual to help his neighbor, but not to pauperize him with making him dependent. Independence for every person is the capitalist ideal.

When a person contracts to work for a day, a week, or a month before he is paid, he is practicing capitalism. It is a series of contracts for transactions to be completed in the future. Capitalism is promise and fulfillment.

Capitalism offers full employment to those who wish to work. The worker is free to accept a job at any wage he can get. He can join with his fellows in voluntary association to improve his salary and working conditions. He can change jobs or start his own business. He relies on his ability to perform rather than on the coercive power of the State to force his employment.

Capitalism is color-blind. Black, brown, yellow, red and white are alike in the marketplace. A person is regarded for his ability rather than his race. Economic rewards in the marketplace, like honor and acclaim on the playing field, are proportionate to performance. The person who has the most skill, ability and ingenuity to produce is paid accordingly by the people who value and need his goods and services.

Trust in the Market

Capitalism is a belief that nobody is wise enough and knows enough to control the lives of other people. When each person buys, sells, consumes, produces, saves, and spends at will, what Leonard Read calls "the miracle of the market" enables everyone to benefit.

Capitalism respects the market as the only effective and fair means of allocating scarce goods. A free market responds to shortages and spurs production by rising prices. Arbitrary controls merely accept and keep the shortages. When rising prices inspire human ingenuity to invent and produce, the goods return and prices fall.

Nobody knows enough to build an airplane or a computer, but hundreds of people working together perform these amazing acts of creation. This is the notable human achievement which Adam Smith called "The Division of Labor."

Capitalism derives its name from the fact that capital is essential to the success of any venture whether it involves an individual, a corporation, or a nation-state. Capital is formed by thrift. The person who accumulates capital is personally rewarded and, at the same time, is a public benefactor.

Capitalism makes every person a trustee of what he has. It appoints him general manager of his own life and property, and it holds him responsible for that trusteeship.

Church and Family Ties

Capitalism is a natural ally of religion. The Judeo-Christian doctrines of stewardship and vocation are reflected in a free market economy. Churches and synagogues can be free and thriving with capitalism. When the churches falter, the moral strength of capitalism is diminished.

Capitalism depends on the family for much of its social and moral strength. When the family disintegrates, the capitalist order falls into confusion and disarray. The motive power for the pursuit of life, liberty, and property is in the filial and parental love of a home with its dimensions of ancestry and posterity.

Capitalism enables entrepreneurs to be free people, taking their own risks and collecting their own rewards.

Work is a privilege and a virtue under capitalism. Leisure is honored, but idleness is suspect. The idea that work is a scourge and a curse has no place in the climate of capitalism.

Capitalism holds profits derived from risk and investment to be as honorable as wages or rent. Dividends paid to those who invest capital in an enterprise are as worthy as interest paid to a depositor in a savings bank. The idea abroad that risk capital is unproductive is patently false.

The Voluntary Way

Capitalism honors and promotes charity and virtue. True charity cannot be compelled. Universities, hospitals, social agencies, are more satisfactory and more fun when they derive from voluntary support. Money taken by force and bestowed by formula is no gift.

The consumer is sovereign under capitalism. No bureaucrat, marketing expert, advertiser, politician, or self-appointed protector can tell him what to buy, sell, or make.

Capitalism encourages invention, innovation and technological advance. Creativity cannot be legislated. Only free people can bring significant discovery to society. Thomas A. Edison was not commissioned by the government.

The concept of free and private enterprise applies to learning and living as well as to the production of goods and services. When a student learns anything it is his own. Nobody, let alone a state, ever taught anybody anything. The State can compel conformity of a sort, but genuine learning is an individual matter—an act of free enterprise and discovery.

Respect for the Individual

Capitalism honors the liberty and dignity of every person. The private citizen is not regarded as a stupid dupe to every crook and con man. He is regarded as a free citizen under God and under the law—able to make his own choices; not a ward of the State who must be protected by his self-appointed superiors who administer government offices.

Capitalism is a system which distributes power to the worker, the young, the consumer, and the disadvantaged by offering freedom for voluntary organization, dissent, change, choice, and political preference, without hindrance from the police power of government.

The renewal of capitalism could be the renewal of America; nothing could be more radical, more timely, or more beneficial to the responsible and trustworthy common people who are now beguiled by the soft and seductive promises of the new socialism.

No political and economic system is perfect. Plato's *Republic* was in heaven—not on earth. If people were all generous and good, any system would work. Since people are self-centered, they are more free and happy in a system which allows the avarice and aggressiveness of each to serve the best interest of all. Capitalism is such a system. It is modestly effective even in chains. The time has come for daring people to release it and let us once more startle the world with the initiative and productivity of free people!

Some of my academic colleagues will deny, dispute, or scorn the foregoing laudatory comments about capitalism. They will say that socialism benefits the poor, the young, the consumer, the minorities, and that capitalism protects the rich and the powerful. When discussion is joined, however, they will argue in terms of politics rather than economics, ideology rather than empirical evidence, and they will accuse me of doing the same. When the most persuasive case is produced, it will not convince. Political opinions are not changed by rational argument.

A Call for Renewal

Those who have socialist ideological preferences are merely annoyed to arrogance and disdain by such honest appreciation of capitalism as I have presented. Those scholars, however, who like Ludwig von Mises, Friedrich Hayek, and Milton Friedman have explored the relevance of capitalism to our present predicament, will join in the call for renewal of a system that works. Those who, like the late Joseph Schumpeter, have watched the apparently relentless disintegration of capitalism, and have concluded that socialism will work, albeit with painful disadvantages, will heave a long, sad sigh of regret at the passing of the happy and prosperous capitalist way of life. They will, as people must, accept what appears from their perspective inevitable, and try to make the best of the gray and level life of socialism.

Schumpeter, however, was no defeatist. He was a perceptive

analyst of human affairs. In the preface to the second edition of his *magnum opus* he wrote, "This, finally, leads to the charge of 'defeatism.' I deny entirely that this term is applicable to a piece of analysis. Defeatism denotes a certain psychic state that has meaning only in reference to action. Facts in themselves and inferences from them can never be defeatist or the opposite whatever that might be. The report that a given ship is sinking is not defeatist. Only the spirit in which this report is received can be defeatist: The crew can sit down and drink. But it can also rush to the pumps."[2]

Friends of liberty, to the pumps!

Those who love liberty more than equality, those who are uneasy with unlimited government, those who have faith in man's ability to shape his own destiny, those who have marveled at the miracle of the market will join me in this call for renewal of this simple, reasonable, versatile, and open system of capitalism which has worked, is working, and will work if freed from the fetters of limitless state intervention. The choice, I believe, is ours. The alternative is the stifling sovereign state.

---

1. John Kenneth Galbraith, *Economics and the Public Purpose* (Boston: Houghton Mifflin Company, 1973), p. 277.
2. Joseph Schumpeter, *Capitalism, Socialism and Democracy* (New York: Harper and Row, 1950), p. xi.

Laissez Faire

by Garet Garrett

The Shivering Ghost that now inhabits the words *laissez faire* was once an unconquerable fighting spirit. It did not belong to capitalism. It belonged to liberty; and to this day its association with capitalism is valid only insofar as capitalism represents liberty.

When the great struggle for individual liberty began in Europe, the one interest that controlled the life of the mind was religion. What men wanted most of all was freedom to worship God in their own way, freedom to believe or disbelieve; and for that they went to death at the stake intoning their hymns of heresy. The religious wars were terrible. They lasted until the lust of fanaticism was sated. Then reason rebelled and there was peace, founded on the principle of *laissez faire* in religion. That is not what anyone called it at that time, because the words had not yet been invented; but that is what it was. Thereafter, so far as religion was concerned, the individual was to be let alone.

Great transactions of the human spirit have momentum, displacement, and direction, but no sharp edges; there is no sudden passage from one time to another. Long after the principle of *laissez faire* had been accepted in Europe, religious tyranny continued. Men were free to join any church they liked, but if they chose, for example, to be Calvinists, they found themselves enthralled again by a discipline that claimed jurisdiction not only over their souls but over their everyday life and all their economic behavior.

The next phase of the great European struggle for liberty, therefore, was aimed at freedom of enterprise. To say that religious radicalism was followed by economic radicalism is merely to make a statement of chronological fact. How were the two things re-

---

Garet Garrett (1878–1954) was the author of over a dozen books, and held numerous writing positions, including financial reporter for the *Wall Street Journal* and chief editorial writer of the *Saturday Evening Post.*

This article first appeared in the Winter 1949 issue of *American Affairs* and was reprinted in the April 1964 issue of *The Freeman.*

lated? Were they but two aspects of one thing? In the preface to *Religion and the Rise of Capitalism,* R. H. Tawney says:

> . . . the existence of a connection between economic radicalism and religious radicalism was to those who saw both at first-hand something not far from a platitude. Until some reason is produced for rejecting their testimony, it had better be assumed that they knew what they were talking about. How precisely that connection should be conceived is, of course, a different question. It had, obviously, two sides. Religion influenced, to a degree which today is difficult to appreciate, men's outlook on society. Economic and social changes acted powerfully on religion.

The universal habit of mind was biblical. People whose fathers and grandfathers had been tortured, burned at the stake, and buried alive for the offense of reading Scripture for themselves might be expected, when they did read it, to construe it literally and in a grim manner. They did. Bunyan's *Pilgrim's Progress* was the authentic account of what happened to the righteous spirit in its passage through this world to the next. The poor were friends of God. They knew for sure they would not meet the rich man in the Kingdom of Heaven. Avarice was a deadly sin. Pursuit of gain was the way to damnation. Moneychangers, speculators, and traders had always about them that certain odor that came from supping with Satan. To buy cheap and sell dear was extortion. Land was the only honorable form of wealth. Business was the ignoble part of the social anatomy.

The Age of Discovery

But the world had something to say for itself, and the world, too, had something to believe. Somehow, for the first time in the history of human thought, the idea of progress had appeared. It was the Age of Discovery. Knowledge was increasing; and this was not revealed knowledge of things hereafter, but knowledge of things here and now. After all, since everybody had to pass through this world whether he liked it or not, why shouldn't man improve his environment if he could by the practical application of knowledge? Although no one understood them clearly, although there was no such word as economics, great economic changes were taking place, and the realities were uncontrollable.

The religious mind stood in a bad dilemma. It could sense the oncoming world, almost as if it had a premonition of the modern era, and yet it had no way of meeting it and was in fact forbidden by the Bible to meet it at all. Thus it became involved in extreme contradictions. For example, to lend money at interest was un-Christian. For money to earn money was usury, and usury was sin. Yet as the necessities of trade increased, the economic function of the moneylender was one that somehow had to be performed, with the result that the Jews were brought in to do for Christians what Christians were morally unable to do for themselves. That is one of the reasons why the Jews became the great moneylenders of Europe.

The question was: Could Bunyan's hero, Christian, become an economic man and at the same time save his soul? The Dutch were the first to say positively yes, and this was significant, because the Dutch had paid more for religious liberty than any other people. They had carried their struggle for it to a plane of appalling heroism. Sooner than yield, they were willing to accept total doom. Their resistance so infuriated the Holy Office of the Inquisition that on February 16, 1568, *all the inhabitants of the Netherlands* were sentenced to death as heretics and Bible readers, except only a few persons especially named in the edict. In Motley's classic, *The Rise of the Dutch Republic*, one may read that—

> Men in the highest positions were daily and hourly dragged to the stake. Alva, in a single line to Philip, coolly estimates the number of executions which were to take place immediately after the expiration of the Holy week at 800 heads.

Tolerance and Trade

If the spirit of *laissez faire* had been less than immortal, it could never have passed through that valley of death. What emerged was the Dutch Republic, founded on the ashes of its martyrs, dedicated to liberty of conscience, holding aloft a light for the world.

Then an amazing thing happened. The prosperity of Holland became the wonder and envy of Europe. In the trade of the world it advanced to first place, and took what Tawney calls the role of economic schoolmaster to seventeenth-century Europe.

The power of individualism now for the first time was released to perform its examples. The result was that tolerance and trade flourished together.

The English came to it slowly and roundabout. Calvinism as they had got it from Geneva was a severe and rigid doctrine. It perceived very clearly that the three aspects of man were spiritual, political, and economic; but since in two of these aspects he was wicked, or much tempted to be, the church was obliged not only to mind his soul but to impose severe discipline upon his political and economic activities. Its regulation of business was medieval and precise; it made ethical and social laws to govern such matters as the use of capital, usury, the just price, profits, the profit motive itself, wages, labor relations, contracts, and trade agreements.

It remained for the Puritans of England to make the great rational construction of this doctrine. They could not understand why God should not admire success in work. Was not the universe his work? Why not suppose that the plan of its just order required his children to work and to succeed? If in moneymaking there were spiritual hazards, then all the more reason for keeping it straight with God. The way to do that was to put God in the shop. Where else could one be so sure of his presence and blessing? In the Puritan doctrine the word "calling" was one of special meaning: "God doth call every man and woman to serve in some peculiar employment, both for their own and the common good." There was a spiritual calling and a temporal calling. The Christian's duty was to take part in the practical affairs of the world, and to succeed in the world could be only a sign that God witnessed his work and was pleased with it. If riches were added to him that, too, would be to the glory of God. In any case, he would never be idle rich, like Dives. Whether riches were good or bad was a question to be settled between the rich man and God; but idleness, thriftlessness, and profligacy were positive evils.

So it was that in the Puritan creed religious liberty and economic freedom were reconciled. The church would let business alone and trust God in the shop to keep it from evil.

Political Freedom and the Industrial Revolution

The next struggle was to get business free from the restrictions imposed upon it by government, not in the name of morals, but in the name of policy.

When that stormy cape had been rounded, the victory of *laissez faire* was complete, and the way was open for that great outburst of European energy which brought on the Industrial Revolution, led by England.

The medieval epoch was finished. Individualism was exalted to a way of life. The foundations of modern capitalism were laid. The powers of government were limited. Free enterprise began. In pursuit of his economic ends, on his way to transform the world, European man was released from the restraints and sanctions imposed upon him both by the ecclesiastical tyranny and a vast bureaucratic system of administrative law. Looking at it later when most of the consequences were already clear, Montesquieu, the French philosophical historian, said "the English had progressed furthest of all people in three important things—piety, commerce, and freedom."

That would have been about 1750. For more than 200 years the spirit of *laissez faire* had been acting irresistibly, and yet that name for it was not known. The words had been used by the Physiocrats in 1736 in France, but hardly anywhere else—nor were they familiar to anybody in England when sixty years later, in 1810, a Commission in the House of Commons said:

> No interference of the legislature with the freedom of trade and with the perfect liberty of each individual to dispose of his time or of his labor in the way or on the terms which he may judge most conducive to his own interest, can take place without violating general principles of the first importance to the prosperity and happiness of the community.

Practice Precedes Principle

In those words government, the British government at least, renounced the right to touch business at all. No more forthright statement of the doctrine of *laissez faire* has perhaps ever been written. Mark, however, that the words do not appear in that statement. They were of French origin, written at first *laissez nous faire*, meaning, "let us alone," and then *laissez faire*, meaning, "let it be." They expressed a philosophic idea. The idea was that the movements of society were spontaneous, not artificial, and that if you let them alone the results in the end, or, as the economist now says, in the long run, would be better for society as a whole—the idea, that is, of a natural order in which there is implicit harmony between public and private interest.

The point is that the spirit of *laissez faire* had already brought into the world religious liberty and freedom of enterprise, and that the foundations of what now may be called *laissez-faire* capitalism had already been laid before the words were familiar or had any epithetical meaning.

"Wealth of Nations"

Most people would probably say that the bible of *laissez-faire* capitalism was written by Adam Smith. His *Wealth of Nations* appeared in 1776. Since some French economists had been using the term for forty years, Adam Smith must have heard it, and yet in the index to *Wealth of Nations* (Cannan Edition) you will find no reference to it. Then people say, "Yes, but it is implicit," and ask you to remember the famous passage about the invisible hand. In the index to the *Wealth of Nations* there is a reference to that passage and it reads as follows:

> If each individual, therefore, endeavors as much as he can both to employ his capital in the support of domestic industry and so to direct that industry that its products may be of the greatest of value, each individual necessarily labors to render the annual revenue of society as great as he can. He generally, indeed, neither intends to promote the public interest or knows how much he is promoting it . . . he intends only his own gain, and he is in this, as in many other cases, led by an invisible hand to promote an end which was not part of his intention. Nor is it always the worse for society that it was not part of it. By pursuing his own interest he frequently promotes that of society more effectually than when he really intends to promote it. I have never known much good was done by those who affected to trade for the public good.

You may take that to express the doctrine of economic *laissez faire*, but the true meaning goes far beyond economics and belongs to the philosophy of individualism, founded upon the faith that man's spontaneous works will be more than his reason can explain. Adam Smith did not invent that philosophy, nor in his exposition of it did he surpass others who wrote before him, notably Adam Ferguson, who said:

> Nations stumble upon establishments which are indeed the results of human action but not the result of human design.

Poetically, the same thought was expressed in Mandeville's *Fable of the Bees.* More than a century before Adam Smith's time, John Moore was saying in England:

> It is an undeniable maxim that everyone by the light of nature and reason will do that which makes for his greatest advantage. . . . The advancement of private persons will be the advantage of the public.

Twenty years after the *Wealth of Nations* appeared, Edmund Burke, another great exponent of individualism, was referring to:

> . . . the benign and wise disposer of all things who obliges men, whether they will or not, in pursuing their own selfish interests, to connect the general good with their own individual success.

He need not have got that from Adam Smith, for *laissez faire* by that time was already ascendant in the economic world, its principles were known and its works were observable.

Objections to Laissez Faire

Nearly 150 years ago Sismondi and his friends, evolving the theory of state socialism, were attacking *laissez faire* on four points, namely:

1. That the fancied harmony between private and public interest did not in fact exist, wherefore liberty of the individual to pursue his own economic advantage would leave *human needs* in the lurch;

2. That it would lead to *serious inequalities* in the distribution of wealth;
3. That it elevated *materialism* and *success*; and
4. That it involved society in such *society catastrophes* as *mass unemployment*.

And all of this was before steamships, railroads, electricity, gasoline, motor cars, automatic machines, or mass production—even before there was such a thing in the world as a piece of farm machinery.

At that time all economic and political thought in Europe was basically pessimistic. Nobody could imagine that in the next few generations, under *laissez-faire* capitalism, consumable wealth would be so prodigiously multiplied that the luxuries of the rich in one generation would become the necessary satisfactions of the poor in the next, and that from time to time surplus—a strange word for an incredible thing—would be the superficial cause of economic depression and unemployment. There had never been surplus before. There had never been too much of anything. Poverty was thought to be permanent and irreducible.

Inroads Against Poverty

The idea that poverty could be abolished did not arise in Europe. That was an American idea. And it could arise here, not because this country was rich in natural resources, but because here the conditions of *laissez-faire* capitalism were more nearly realized than anywhere else in the world. Under stress of unlimited and uncontrolled competition we made the discovery that broke Europe's "iron law of wages"—the law, namely, that since wages were paid out of the profits of capital, the wage fund was limited by the capital fund, and the capital fund was something that could be increased only in a slow and painful manner by limiting consumption.

We discovered that wages were not paid out of profits. They were paid out of production. Therefore, wages and profits could rise together, if only you increased production. Moreover, production itself created capital, as in the Ford example—the example of a company that began with $28,000 in cash and at the end of forty-five years employed in its work $1 billion of capital, all its own and all created out of production. And this was done by making the motor car so cheap that almost nobody was too poor to be able to possess and enjoy it.

American Capitalism

Those who speak of capitalism as if it were in itself a kind of universal order, with hierarchy, creed, and orthodoxy, are either unable to make distinctions or find that distinctions inconvenience their argument. Capitalism takes its character from the soil and climate in which it grows. American capitalism is so unlike European capitalism that the two could hardly be transplanted. Why has American capitalism been so much more productive than capitalism anywhere else? The seed was European. The sapling was not. Why did this one tree grow to a size and a fruitfulness so prodigious that all the people of the world come begging for its windfall?

There was here neither skill nor knowledge not possessed also by the people in Europe. Yet after five generations, with less than one-tenth of the earth's land area and less than one-fifteenth of its total population, we have now [1949] in our hands one-half of the industrial power of the whole world. Europe's star did not fall. That is not what happened. The American star dimmed it out. What made that difference between our creative power and that of Europe?

The difference was that here the magic of liberty was acting as it never had acted anywhere before.

Until the American Declaration of Independence, said Lord Acton, the history of freedom would have been "a history of the thing that was not."

American capitalism not only has been the most successful in the world; it is the one great citadel of economic freedom surviving and now carries the burden of defending Christian civilization against its Eastern enemy. From this it follows that when you compare capitalism with communism, the comparison is in fact between American capitalism, with its Puritan tradition, and Russian communism, which is uncompromisingly materialistic and atheistic.

The two ancient enemies of *laissez faire* were the state and the church. *Laissez faire* represented the principle of radicalism in both religion and economics. Radicalism was the sword of liberty. Neither the state nor the church has ever loved liberty. Now, what was conservative is radical, and *laissez faire*, which was radical, is reactionary. The wheel has gone all the way around.

Morality in America

by Norman S. Ream

Early in the nineteenth century the brilliant French observer Alexis de Tocqueville gave this estimate of America and Americans in his book *Democracy in America:* "There is no country in the world where the Christian religion retains a greater influence over the souls of men than America."

A similar assessment could not be made at the end of the twentieth century. That is not to say that the Christian religion exercises any great influence over the souls of men in any nation today, but the loss of its original influence is certainly as great if not greater in the United States than anywhere else. Substitute the words "morality" or "ethics" for the words "Christian religion" and their influence would still be seriously questionable. One might perhaps even put it this way and not be far from the truth: *There is no country in the world where the Christian religion has lost more of its moral influence over the souls of men than in America.*

The high moral principles of the Christian religion have been corrupted by greed and envy, and greed and envy have caused and been exacerbated by the very programs America's politicians have adopted in a misguided effort to eliminate poverty and inequalities of all kinds. It is impossible to have both liberty and equality, for the attempt to achieve the latter will always destroy the former. When government assures its citizens that they are entitled to be equal it does two things: It levels by pulling down those at the top, and it engenders greed and envy in those at the bottom.

There was once a commonly observed moral philosophy or moral culture in America, but that is no longer true. Today Americans have few generally held convictions concerning good and evil, right and wrong, morality and immorality. In part it is the consequence of our heterogeneous population resulting from the

---

Dr. Ream, who served for many years as pastor of the First Congregational Church, Wauwatosa, Wisconsin, lives in retirement with his wife in Estes Park, Colorado. This article appeared in the July 1993 issue of *The Freeman*.

vast numbers of immigrants from countries of different cultures. Those who had been so anxious to come to America and enjoy its blessings have often brought with them philosophies and cultures inimical to those held by earlier settlers. As a consequence they have helped destroy the very blessings they sought. But the descendants of those earlier settlers have abandoned their forebears' beliefs, and this has been a major factor in the waning of Christianity and ethics in America.

The generally held moral principles which once guided human action in America had their roots in the Christian religion as Tocqueville pointed out. One can argue that the Founding Fathers did not always agree in their interpretation of that religion—some were deists—but the great majority of them drew their moral and ethical guidelines from the Ten Commandments and the teachings and example of Jesus of Nazareth. They were of one mind in their conviction that there should be freedom of religion for all.

Religious Beliefs of the Founders

The most orthodox and ardent believer among the principal figures urging freedom from the constraints of England and King George III was Samuel Adams, who with other Sons of Liberty dumped the tea into Boston Harbor. A stern Calvinist, he believed liberty was dependent on the moral and spiritual principles enunciated in the New Testament. In a letter to John Scollay in 1776 he wrote,

> Revelation assures us that Righteousness exalteth a nation—Communities are dealt with in this world by the wise and just Ruler of the Universe. He rewards or punishes them according to their general character. The diminution of public virtue is usually attended with that of public happiness, and the public liberty will not long survive the total extinction of morals.

At the other extreme, if it can be called extreme, was the deist Thomas Paine, whom Theodore Roosevelt is once said to have referred to as a "filthy little atheist." In 1797, however, Paine started a movement in Paris to combat atheism. He did not believe in revelation nor did he believe the Bible was divinely inspired, but in the *Prospect Papers*, published in 1804 by Elihu Palmer, he wrote: "It is by the exercise of our reason that we are enabled to contemplate God in His works and imitate Him in His way. When we see His care and goodness extended over all His creatures, it teaches us our duty toward each other, while it calls forth our gratitude to Him."

The idea that many if not most of the Founding Fathers were atheists or agnostics is incorrect. Not only were they devoutly religious, but they firmly believed that liberty and justice depended on an observance of the moral and ethical demands of the Christian religion.

Benjamin Franklin wrote to Ezra Stiles in 1790 that "As to Jesus of Nazareth, my opinion of whom you particularly desire, I think the system of morals and His religion, as he left them to us, the best the world ever saw or is likely to see. . . ."

It was Franklin who urged the delegates to the Constitutional Convention to begin the sessions with prayer: "I have lived, Sir, a long time, and the longer I live, the more convincing proofs I see of this truth—that God governs in the affairs of men. And if a sparrow cannot fall to the ground without His notice, is it probable that an empire can rise without his aid?"

Our first president, George Washington, rarely spoke of his religious beliefs but on one occasion wrote a letter to the Philadelphia-area clergy in which he stated his conviction that "Religion and morality are the essential pillars of Civil society. . . ." In his Farewell Address he declared, "Of all the dispositions and habits which lead to political prosperity, Religion and morality are indispensable supports."

When he took the oath of office in New York, Washington did so with his hand on the Bible and afterward bent down and kissed the book.

Washington's successor in office, John Adams, in an 1810 letter to Benjamin Rush wrote, ". . . religion and virtue are the only foundations, not only of republicanism and of all free government but of social felicity under all governments and in all the combinations of human society."

Alexander Hamilton believed it was man's relationship to God that gave birth to man's natural rights: "The Supreme Being . . . endowed him with rational faculties, by the help of which to discern and pursue such things as were consistent with an inviolable right to personal liberty and personal safety."

Thus did the Founding Fathers state in various ways their firm conviction that a nation desiring individual freedom and national prosperity must be guided by high standards of morality and ethics and that such a moral philosophy could only grow out of a strong religious faith.

The Dissolution of Moral and Ethical Standards

Something has happened to the soul of America and millions of Americans know that what has happened is not good. Even some politicians recognize it and try to convince the electorate that the answer lies in the political arena. The answer, however, is certainly not to be found there. Politics is merely a reflection of the moral and ethical principles of society at large.

We have been urged over and over again by certain individuals and groups to become a value-free society, and that in large part is what we have become. A recent candidate for high office in Colorado insisted, as have many others, that values should not be taught in the public schools. One is tempted to ask if cheating should be acceptable and whether the purpose of public schools is to dump graduates into the work force with no concern for their character and integrity.

Today, lacking any commonly held moral and ethical principles, the test for government activity is not "is it moral and right?" but "is it politically expedient?" Instead of applying the test of sound morality and sound economic principles, political activity is tested by the reactions and pressures of minority groups. There is little distinction any more between morality and legality. Politically inspired legislation makes something right or wrong merely because it is the law and not because it is in harmony with eternal principles tested by 2,000 years of history. John Quincy Adams voiced the truth held by the Founding Fathers:

> This principle, that a whole nation has a right to do whatever it pleases, cannot in any sense whatever be admitted as true. The eternal and immutable laws of justice and morality are paramount to a legislation. The violations of those laws is certainly within the power of a nation, but is not among the rights of nations.

The late Leonard Read, founder of The Foundation for Economic Education, was fond of saying that "Economics is a branch of moral philosophy." He was right, of course, but he could have gone further. The attempt to separate economics, political activity, or any other field from sound principles of morality is to guarantee failure. No policy or program which fails morally can be ultimately successful. Take for example our huge national debt. It is immoral to foist upon future generations a burden caused by our own profligacy. We are now beginning to see the grave consequences of that immorality. The recent situation in California where employees of the state were being paid in IOU's is but a small foretaste of what will almost certainly happen elsewhere.

The Founding Fathers were strongly in favor of religious freedom for all citizens and wanted no religious test for those seeking federal office. Many of those early statesmen were indeed unorthodox in their religion, but they nevertheless were strongly of the opinion that without belief in a divine Creator and in the basic moral and ethical teachings of Jesus no lasting freedom in America could be achieved. They never rejected God nor lost their respect for religion. Moral man and religious man could not be separated.

As Washington, Adams, and Madison knew, morality springs out of religious faith and a people with little or no Christian theology will have a seriously impaired moral philosophy. That leaves us with an important insight regarding the direction in which America and Americans should go.

The crisis facing America and Americans today is not an economic nor a political one. It is a moral and spiritual crisis. It is a crisis of character which has produced a crisis of behavior. It is a poverty of values caused by a poverty of faith. We remove all value judgments from society and then wonder why we have a generation that is morally confused.

Our society has continually and increasingly dismissed the relevance of religion and as a consequence has for masses of people diminished its importance. If religion is ignored or banned then its components such as the Ten Commandments and the teachings of Jesus are likewise made irrelevant and we arrive at the conclusion that "if there is no God then anything is permissible." It is difficult to believe there are many who will rejoice in such a culmination.

The Parable of the Talents: The Bible and Entrepreneurs

by Robert A. Sirico

The parables of Jesus teach eternal truths, but they also offer surprising practical lessons for worldly affairs. In the Gospel According to St. Matthew (chapter 25, verses 14-30) we find Jesus' Parable of the Talents. As with all the biblical parables, it has many layers of meaning. Its essence relates to how we are to use God's gift of grace. As regards the material world, it is a story about capital, investment, entrepreneurship, and the proper use of scarce economic resources. It is a direct rebuttal to those who see a contradiction between business success and living the Christian life.

A rich man who was going on a long journey called his three servants together. He told them they would be caretakers of his property while he was gone. The master had carefully assessed the natural abilities of each servant. He gave five talents to one servant, two to another, and one to the third—to each according to his ability. The master then left on his journey.

The servants went forth into a world open to enterprise and investment. The servant who had received five talents went into business and made five more. The servant who received two made two more. But the servant who received one hid the master's property in a hole in the ground.

The master returned to settle his accounts. The servant who had received five talents came forth. "My lord," he said, "you entrusted me with five talents; see, I have made five more!"

"Well done, good and faithful servant!" the master responded. "You have been faithful over a little, I will set you over much. Enter into the joy of your lord!"

Then the servant who had been given two talents approached the master. "My lord," he said, "you entrusted me with two tal-

Paulist Father Robert A. Sirico is president of the Acton Institute for the Study of Religion and Liberty in Grand Rapids, Michigan. This article originally appeared in the July 1994 issue of *The Freeman*.

ents; see, I have made two talents more!" The master praised the servant in a like manner.

Then the one who had been given one talent approached his master. "My lord," he said, "I knew you to be a hard man; you reap where you have not sown, and gather where you have not scattered; and being afraid I went and hid your talent in the ground. See, you have what is yours!"

The master's response was swift and harsh: "You wicked and indolent slave! You were aware that I reap where I have not sown, and gather where I have not scattered; you ought for that reason to have invested my money with the bankers; then, on my return, I should have received my own with interest."

The master ordered that the talent be taken away from the lazy servant and given to the one with the ten talents. "For to every one who possesses not," said the master, "even that which he has shall be taken away. Cast that useless slave into the outer darkness; there shall be weeping and the grinding of teeth!"

This is not a story we often hear from the pulpit. Our times still exalt a socialist ethic where making a profit is suspect, and entrepreneurship is frowned upon. Yet the story relays a readily apparent ethical meaning, and even deeper lessons for understanding human accountability in economic life.

A Closer Look

The word "talent" in this parable has two meanings. It is a monetary unit: it was the largest denomination of the time. Biblical scholar John R. Donovan, S.J., tells us a single talent was equivalent to the wage of an ordinary worker for fifteen years. So we know the amount given to each servant was considerable.

More broadly interpreted, the talents refer to all of the various gifts God has given us for our use. This definition embraces all gifts—natural, spiritual, and material. It includes our natural abilities and resources—our health, education—as well as our possessions, money, and opportunities.

One of the simplest lessons from this parable is that it is not immoral to profit from our resources, wit, and labor. The alternative to profit is loss, and surely the loss of wealth, especially when due to a lack of initiative, does not constitute good stewardship.

St. Matthew's parable presupposes a local understanding of the proper stewardship of money. According to rabbinical law, burying was regarded as the best security against theft. If a person entrusted with money buried it as soon as he had it in his possession, he would be free from liability if anything should happen to it. The opposite was true for money that was tied in a cloth. In this case, the person was responsible for covering any loss incurred due to the inadequate care of the deposit.

Yet in this story, the master turned this understanding on its head. He considered burying the talent—and thus breaking even—to be a loss, because he thought that capital ought to earn a reasonable rate of return. In this understanding, time is money (or interest).

The parable also contains a critical lesson about how we are to use our God-given capacities and resources. In the book of Genesis God gave Adam the earth with which to mix his labor for his own use. In the parable, in a similar manner, the master expected his servants to seek material gain. Rather than passively preserve what they have been given, they were expected to invest the money. The master was angered at the timidity of the servant who had received the one talent. God commands us to use our talents towards productive ends. The parable emphasizes the need for work and creativity as opposed to idleness.

The Quest for Security

Throughout history, people have tried to construct institutions to provide perfect security, as the failed servant did. Such efforts range from the Greco-Roman welfare states, to full-scale Soviet totalitarianism, to the Luddite communes of the 1960s. From time to time, these efforts have been embraced as Christian solutions to future insecurities. Yet in the Parable of the Talents, courage in the face of an unknown future is rewarded in the first servant, who has been given the most. He had traded the five talents, and in doing so, acquired five more. It would have been safer for the servant to have invested the money in the bank to receive interest. For his faith in his master he is allowed to keep what had been entrusted to him and what he earned, and he is invited to rejoice with the master.

This implies a moral obligation to confront uncertainty in an enterprising way. No one does this better than the entrepreneur. Long before he knows if there will be a return on his investments or ideas, he risks his time and property. He must pay out wages long before he has any idea if he has accurately predicted future events. He looks to the future with courage and a sense of opportunity. In creating new enterprises he opens up alternatives for workers to choose among in earning a wage and developing skills.

Why, then, are entrepreneurs so often castigated as poor servants of God? Many religious leaders speak and act as if the businessman's use of his natural talents and resources to turn a profit is immoral, a notion that should be cast aside in light of the Parable of the Talents. The lazy servant could have avoided his dismal fate by being more entrepreneurial. If he had made an effort to trade with his master's money and came back with less than a talent, he would not have been treated so harshly, for he would have labored on behalf of his master.

Entrepreneurship and Greed

Religion must begin to recognize entrepreneurship for what it is—a vocation. The ability to succeed in business, stock trading, or investment banking is a talent. Like other gifts, it should not be squandered, but used to its fullest for the glory of God. Critics link capitalism with greed, yet the fundamental nature of the entrepreneurial vocation is to focus on the needs of customers. To succeed, the entrepreneur must serve others.

Greed is a spiritual hazard that threatens us all, regardless of our wealth or vocation. The term has a proportional element, meaning there is an *excessive* or *insatiable* desire for material gain, regardless of financial status. The desire is excessive when, in the depths of a person's being, it outweighs moral and spiritual concerns. This parable makes very clear that wealth as such is not unjust—for the first servant received more than the second and third. And when turning a profit is the goal of using the entrepreneurial talent, it is not greed. It is the proper use of the gift.

In addition to condemning profit, religious leaders often favor varieties of social leveling and redistribution of income. Universal health care, greater social welfare spending, and higher taxes on the rich are all promoted in the name of Christian ethics. The ultimate goal of such constructs is equality, as if the inequalities that exist among people are somehow inherently unjust. Yet this is not how Jesus tells it in the Parable of the Talents. The master entrusted to each of his servants talents according to his ability. One received five, while another received only one. The one who received the least does not receive sympathy from the master for his lack of resources in comparison to what his colleagues have been given.

We can infer from this parable, that the leveling of money or the reallocation of resources is not a proper moral concern. The individual talents and raw materials that each of us has are not inherently unjust; there will always be rampant inequalities among people. A moral system is one which recognizes this and allows each person to use his or her talents to the fullest. We all have the responsibility to employ the faculties with which we have been endowed.

We can also apply the lesson of this parable to our nation's social policy. In our existing system, the labor of workers is taxed to provide support for many who do not work. We often hear that there are "no jobs" for many of our poor. Yet there is always work to be done. A man with two working hands can find work for a dollar an hour. He makes a decision not to work. Moreover, our welfare system discourages work. It creates the perverse incentive to go on welfare unless there is a job that will pay at least as much as government relief. God commands all people to use the talents they have been given, yet in the name of charity our welfare system encourages people to let their natural skills atrophy, or keeps them from discovering their talents at all.

We encourage sin this way. The Parable of the Talents implies that inactivity—or wasting entrepreneurial talent—incites the wrath of God. After all, the lowly servant had not squandered his lord's money; he just hid it in the ground, something that was permissible in rabbinical law. The rapidity of the master's reaction is surprising. He calls him "wicked and slothful" and banishes him forever. Apparently it is not just the servant's sloth that brings such wrath on his head. He has also shown no contrition, and has blamed the master for his timidity. His excuse for not investing the money is that he viewed the master as a hard and exacting man, though he had been given generous resources. Bible scholar John

Meir comments, "Out of fear of failure, he has refused to even try to succeed."

This parable also tells us something about macroeconomics. The master went on his journey leaving behind a total of eight talents; upon his return it has become fifteen. The parable is not the story of a zero-sum gain. One person's gain is not another's expense. The successful trading of the first servant does not hinder the prospects for the third servant. So it is true in the economy of today. Unlike what is so often preached from the pulpit, the success of the rich does not come at the expense of the poor.

If by becoming rich the most successful servant had hurt others, the master would not have praised him. A wise use of resources in investment and saving at interest is not only right from the individual point of view; it helps others in the economy as well. A rising tide lifts all boats, as John Kennedy used to say. Similarly, the wealth of the developed world is not on the backs of developing nations. The Parable of the Talents implies a free and open economy.

Often left-leaning Christians will cite Jesus' words: "How hard it is to enter the Kingdom of God. It is easier for a camel to pass through the needle's eye than for a rich man to enter the Kingdom of God." His disciples were taken aback at this, and wondered then who could be saved. Jesus answers their fears, "For man it is impossible, but not for God." This does not mean that our material success will keep us from heaven, yet it does imply the necessity to order our lives properly before all our material concerns. Our concern for God must come just as the servants thought of their master's interest as they pursued profit. It remains true that for all of our worldly goods and deeds, we rely completely on God to attain salvation.

But for the conduct of economics, we rely heavily on entrepreneurship, investment, risk taking, and the expansion of wealth and prosperity. We should lend a critical eye to the way our culture treats enterprise. Business magazines carry stories of business success all the time. The hero is often the forward-looking, courageous, and cheerful entrepreneur, who is much like the capable servant given five talents. Yet at the same time popular religious faith continues to extol and promote behavior endemic to the idle servant who was banished by the master.

Christianity is often blamed for the failed socialist projects the world over. And in many cases misguided Christians have been involved in building socialist constructs. The lesson of the Parable of the Talents needs to be better understood. The socialist dream is not a moral one. It simply institutionalizes the condemned behavior of the lesser servant. Where God commands creative action, socialism encourages laziness. Where He demands faith and hope in the future, socialism promises a base form of security. Where the Parable of the Talents implies the morality of freedom to trade, invest, and profit, socialism denies it.

All people of faith need to work to close the chasm that exists between religion and economic understanding. Jesus' parable is a good place to begin to incorporate the morality of enterprise and the free market into Christian ethics.

III. ECONOMIC FREEDOM

He Gains Most Who Serves Best

by Paul L. Poirot

"The best offense is a good defense" may be effective strategy in war and various competitive sports to decide winners and losers. But this offense-defense terminology is misleading with reference to free market competition. Voluntary exchange is neither a game nor a war; it is a form of cooperation between buyer and seller to their mutual advantage—as each one determines advantage. So, the rule of the market would run more like this: "He gains most who serves best." A businessman's profits are a measure of his efficiency in the use of scarce and valuable resources to satisfy the most urgent wants of consumers.

Having competed successfully in the market, a property owner seeks to preserve his gains. But the market continues to insist: "He gains most who serves best." In other words, the way to preserve your gains is to keep on serving consumers efficiently; that's the only protection of property the market can offer.

It should be noted here that the market recognizes and accommodates numerous forms of property. Perhaps the most crucial and significant form is the individual's property right in his own person—his freedom to use as he pleases for any peaceful purpose his own ideas and energies and other faculties and possessions. As a self-owning, self-responsible human being, he is free to choose work or leisure, thrift or prodigality, specialization and trade or self-subsistence, formal education or on-his-own, splendor or plain living—anything peaceful, at his own expense. The market is there to serve him to the extent that he serves others: "He gains most who serves best."

In addition to one's right to his own life, the market recognizes and respects other forms of private property. There is the land, the space one occupies to the exclusion of others who have not earned access or been freely invited to share that space. There are the

---

Dr. Poirot, editor emeritus of *The Freeman*, contributed dozens of cogent articles to *The Freeman* while serving as editor from 1956 to 1985. He is retired and lives in Pennsylvania. This article originally appeared in the May 1975 issue of *The Freeman*.

man-made buildings and tools of further production. There is food, clothing, shelter, transportation, medical and dental care, news and other information, books, education, recreation, entertainment, services ranging from strictly unskilled manual labor to the most highly skilled professional help. All these are forms of private property, things owned and controlled by individuals as a consequence of peaceful production and trade—voluntary market transactions, according to the market formula: "He gains most who serves best."

A Wealthy Nation

Those who speak of the United States as a wealthy nation really mean that the citizens of this nation are relatively well off. And we should add the appropriate qualifications: (1) some of the citizens of the United States own more property than do others, and (2) the typical United States citizen owns more property than the typical citizen of other countries.

Without those qualifying conditions, the reference to a wealthy United States might be misconstrued as meaning that our federal government has unlimited resources at its command—an all-too-common belief.

Perhaps the people of the so-called underdeveloped Third World might be excused for the notion that the wealth of the United States is primarily in the form of government property. Citizens of lands long committed to communism have less reason to believe that the path to prosperity and happiness is through government ownership and control of resources. But what could be our excuse, we taxpayers of the United States, for possibly thinking of Uncle Sam as the source of endless goodies? Either our government is independently wealthy and has no need for taxpayers, or else it is dependent on taxpayers for its resources. Is there really any question about that?

Unfortunately, many citizens of the United States seem to be in doubt as to which is the case. They vote themselves instant protection and welfare, payable from federal funds, as if there were no tomorrow—no accompanying tax burdens and disruption of business and trade. The facts to the contrary are announced daily in the various taxes added to purchases, weekly or bi-weekly in the list of deductions from pay checks, annually as income tax reports are filed. We have every reason to know there is a tax to pay for every act of government, whether to defend life and property and maintain peace and assure justice, or to transfer property from one person to another for whatever reason.

Why Some Have More

Because the market rewards individuals according to services rendered, the result is that some persons earn and own more property than do others. Strictly by serving the masses of mankind, some individuals have been made extremely wealthy. They have been given stewardship over vast amounts of property because of their proven capacity to use such scarce resources efficiently in providing the goods and services most sought and most valued by others. But, if for some reason, any present owner of scarce resources loses his touch, fails to serve efficiently, the open competition of the ongoing market process soon will bid the property into the hands of some new owner who serves better.

Meanwhile, the market process sustains vast numbers of us who pretend to *know* better than we *do*—who feign a wisdom not manifest in our performances. And one version of such "wisdom" holds that "we" know better than "they" how to use their property, that there is a more humane and just method of allocating scarce and valuable resources than to leave it to the market decisions of competing owners of private property. In other words, property should be redistributed "to each according to need," not left to the market rule: "He gains most who serves best." And just how is the market to be closed? Forcibly! Instead of upholding the dignity and property rights of the peaceful owner, the government shall intervene sometimes to drag a supplier unwillingly to market, sometimes to bar or limit his entry; sometimes to protect present owners of property in uses long since declared wasteful by any reasonable measure of the market place, sometimes to forcibly transfer property from the most efficient users into the hands of those who most miserably have failed to serve others in any way whatsoever.

The Best System

So we come back once more to the only rule the market follows, "He gains most who serves best." Despite the inequalities of wealth resulting from observance of that rule, no one reasonably contends that there is a better formula for human action in society. There is nothing morally wrong about voluntarily serving others. A person does not rationally contend that he has been impoverished because others have acted to serve his most urgent wants. When two parties voluntarily exchange their privately owned resources or properties, each gains—else he would not trade; and no uninvolved third party is harmed by reason of the trade.

While the rule of the market allows the greatest gain to the one who serves best, it affords no protection for any gain except through continuing use in the efficient service of others. In other words, the market insists that scarce resources be owned by those who are most proficient in serving willing customers, which is the least wasteful social distribution of wealth that is possible. To arbitrarily or coercively change the market-derived pattern of ownership is to introduce waste; and there is no historical or theoretically sound evidence that waste of scarce resources is socially beneficial. What any waste of any scarce resource amounts to in the final analysis is a waste of human lives—the inevitable consequence when compulsory collectivism interferes with or displaces the market process of open competition.

It is comforting to be a citizen of a wealthy nation. But a nation is wealthy only by reason of the fact that resources are privately owned and controlled according to the rule, "He gains most who serves best." And the only way in which government can usefully serve such a society is to keep the market open, restrain and punish those who violate the rule, but otherwise let free men compete.

Markets and Morality

by Peter J. Hill

In terms of sheer ability to provide goods and services, most people would agree that capitalism wins hands down when compared with alternative economic systems such as socialism. Even so, many critics of private property and markets prefer a more socialistic system or at least one that places more power in the hands of the government. They argue that although capitalism delivers the goods in a material sense, it doesn't deliver them morally. That is, capitalism doesn't satisfy certain basic standards of justice.

This article challenges that position by examining several areas where moral issues weigh in on the side of the marketplace. This is not an argument that a society based on free markets is the same as a moral society; people can behave morally or immorally in a free market system just as they can in other systems. However, capitalism does have a number of moral strengths that are lacking in other economic systems.

Although the "market" is often considered an alternative to central planning or state ownership of the means of production, it is not a rigid institutional order like socialism or communism. What we call capitalism or a free-market society is a society based upon private property rights. Individuals may own, buy, and sell property (including their own labor) if they do not do so fraudulently, and they are free to do what they want with their property as long as they do not harm others. Individuals may decide to exchange their property with others, thereby creating a market. This market process is not mandated by anybody and requires only a well-defined and enforced system of private property rights in order to exist.

Inherent in capitalism is the ability to provide freedom of choice, encourage cooperation, provide accountability, create wealth for large numbers of people, and limit the exercise of excessive power.

Dr. Hill is George F. Bennett Professor of Economics at Wheaton College (Illinois) and a senior associate of PERC, a research center in Bozeman, Montana, with whose permission we republish this article. This essay appeared in the February 1989 issue of *The Freeman*.

Freedom of Choice

A market system assumes very little about the ideal way to organize economic life. Other societies may mandate cooperatives, or communes, or cottage industries, or they may prohibit them. But a system of private property offers a wide range of possible forms of organization. If cooperatives are desirable, they can be used; but other forms for organizing production are also permissible. And, in fact, the individual who wishes to ignore the market or construct alternative institutional arrangements is perfectly free to do so.

Throughout history certain groups have chosen to operate largely outside the market. One such group, the Hutterites, lives in the northern Great Plains of the United States and Canada. The more than 200 Hutterite agricultural colonies have been remarkably successful in maintaining their identity and expanding their population. Yet they are far from capitalistic. All property within the Hutterite colony, except the most basic personal items, is owned in common. All income is shared equally within the colony, and no wages are paid for labor.

The Hutterites were able to establish their colonies without prior approval from anyone in society. No committee, government agency, or group of well-meaning citizens had to meet and decide if the Hutterite lifestyle should be allowed. The freedom to choose such alternatives is unique to a free market society.

In contrast, a centrally planned society does not grant freedom to those who want to engage in market transactions. It limits voluntary trade in the interest of some other goal, and undoubtedly would constrain groups like the Hutterites if the people in power disliked the Hutterites' form of organization.

Cooperation vs. Conflict

A free-market, private property system usually is labeled competitive. Yet one of the major advantages of the market system is that it encourages cooperation rather then mere competition. Competition does exist in a market-based system, but competition is prevalent in any society in which scarcity exists.

In the marketplace, successful competitors cooperate with, or satisfy, others in the society. In order to succeed in a private property system, individuals must offer a "better deal" than their competitors. They cannot coerce people to buy their products or services. They must focus their creative impulses and energy on figuring out ways to satisfy others. The person who does this best is the one who succeeds in the market. Thus, participants in a market economy—buyers and sellers—continually look for areas of agreement where they can get along, rather than concentrating unproductively on the areas of disagreement.

In contrast, under a collective order, rewards frequently come from being as truculent and uncompromising as possible. With collective decision-making those in stronger political positions have little reason to look for areas of agreement; generally, they have a better chance to succeed by discrediting the opposition to justify their own position, compromising only when others are strong.

A good example of the dissension caused by collective decision-making is the controversy over teaching the origins of mankind. School boards—which must make collective decisions—generally have to decide to teach either that human beings were created or that they evolved. Such decisions are fraught with conflict. People who disagree with a board's decision march, write letters to the newspaper, lobby, hire lawyers, and, in general, become quite exercised. This is almost inevitable when highly emotional issues are involved since any collective decision, including one made by majority vote, is likely to be contrary to the wishes of a minority. Thus, the decision-makers are in a no-win situation. If the board allows creationism to be taught, evolutionists will be irate. If they decide to teach evolution, creationists will be outraged.

In contrast, consider the decision to be vegetarian or carnivorous. There are individuals who feel every bit as strongly about this issue as those involved in the origins-of-mankind debate. Nevertheless, there is little chance that a decision about diet will generate public controversy. Diet is not determined by a collective decision-making process, so people can interact rather peacefully about it. The person who believes that avoiding meat is healthier or morally correct can pursue such a diet without arguing with the meat eater. Advocates of a meat diet can find producers and grocery stores eager to satisfy their desires. In fact, vegetarians and the meat eaters can shop at the same stores, pushing their carts past each other with no conflict. It is the absence of collective decision-making that permits this peaceful proximity.

The social harmony that results from a market order should be of great interest to those concerned with moral issues. People of very different cultures, values, and world views can live together without rancor under a system of private rights and markets. A market order requires only minimal agreement on personal goals or social end-states.

In contrast, alternative institutional orders are more oriented toward centrally determined goals. The very existence of such orders requires a more general agreement on what is "good" for society. A centrally planned system not relying on willing exchange of work for pay must direct individuals to labor to achieve certain ends, and those ends are not necessarily the same as workers or consumers would choose freely. For instance, in the Soviet Union very little freedom was allowed in occupational choice, and once one had been assigned a job it was very difficult to move to a different one.

Another reason that a system based on private property rights encourages social harmony is that it holds people accountable for what they do to others. Under a private property regime, a person who injures another or damages another's property is responsible for the damages, and courts enforce this responsibility. The mere knowledge that damage must be paid for leads people to act carefully and responsibly. When people are accountable for their actions, individual freedom can be allowed.

In contrast, a centrally planned system holds individuals far less accountable. Although in theory the government is charged with enforcing people's rights, rights in such a system are ill-defined and the government can and does respond to the wishes of powerful people with little regard for the rights or wishes of the powerless. Even in democracies, if government has the power to grant favors, powerful groups try to use the government to take what they want. What they take may have been worth far more to those from whom it was taken.

Zero-Sum vs. Positive-Sum Views of the World

Many objections to private property hinge on income distribution. Well-intentioned people often think that it is unfair for some to live in luxury while others have very little. I am sympathetic to the view that the affluent are morally obligated to share their wealth with those who have less. But that doesn't mean that the state is the appropriate agency for such redistribution.

A significant number of people who object to the relative position of the wealthy do so because of a basic misapprehension about where wealth comes from. They believe that those who live in luxury do so at the expense of others who live in poverty. In general this is not true.

The world is not zero-sum. That is, the wealth of the world is not limited so that it has to be divided up among all, with some people getting more and others getting less. While wealth can be obtained by taking it from others, wealth also can be created by properly motivated human action. When that happens, wealth represents a net addition to the well-being of a society. The significant increases in per capita wealth since the Industrial Revolution have come about primarily through the creation of wealth, not by taking from others.

Under a set of well-defined and enforced property rights, the *only* transactions people engage in are "positive-sum" or wealth-creating transactions, those that occur because all parties to the transaction believe they will be better off as a result. In a society where people have secure rights to their property, they will exchange property only voluntarily, and they will do so only when they see the potential for improving their situation. The people they are dealing with will do the same—engage in transactions only when they expect to be better off as a result.

A zero-sum world, where one accumulates more wealth solely by decreasing the wealth of others, occurs only in the *absence* of property rights. In such a world people—either by themselves as brigands and thieves or through the use of governmental power—can obtain command over resources without obtaining the consent of the owners of the resources.

Some critics argue that many market transactions are not voluntary, that some people are forced by circumstances to enter into transactions they don't want. For instance, they argue that an employer is exploiting workers by hiring them at the lowest possible wage. Yet in a society in which people act voluntarily, without coercion, the acceptance of such an offer means that no better wages are available. Indeed, the employer is expanding the opportunities for the unfortunate. A law mandating a $4.00 minimum wage, for example, actually decreases the opportunities for those whose work is worth only $2.00.

The only way a government—as opposed to the private sector, which acts through voluntary giving—can help these people is to give them wealth that it takes from someone else. Yet the fact that wealth usually has been created by its owners, not taken from others, weakens the moral case for such redistribution. A person whose creative effort adds to the stock of wealth without decreasing the well-being of others would seem to have a moral claim to that new wealth.

Moreover, under a private property system that relies on the market process, net additions to wealth roughly reflect how much one has added to the wealth of *other* people. In a market system, the only way to become wealthy is to please others, and the way to become very wealthy is to please the masses. Henry Ford catered to the masses with his automobile, satisfying their need for relatively cheap transportation, and he became immensely wealthy. In contrast, Henry Royce chose to serve only those with high incomes by producing an expensive automobile, and he did not become nearly as rich. To penalize people who carry out actions like Henry Ford's by forcibly taking large amounts of their income seems perverse.

Unfortunately, the mistaken zero-sum view of the world is quite prevalent. Many participants in discussions about Third World poverty believe that if only the wealthy nations weren't so well off, the poor nations would be richer. Although it certainly is possible that some of the wealth of some people has been taken from others, this is not usually the case. And if such takings occur, the solution is to move to a regime that protects people's rights to their property.

Ironically, the view that the world is zero-sum often makes conditions worse. Proponents of the zero-sum view usually favor large-scale political reallocation of rights. Such reallocation encourages, indeed requires, that everybody enter the fray. War is expensive whether it occurs on the battlefield or in the halls of Congress. When government has the ability to hand out numerous favors, many citizens compete for these favors, while others lobby vigorously to retain their assets. Typically, the net result is less wealth remaining after reallocation than before reallocation.

Power

The gravest injustices in the history of mankind have occurred when some people have had excessive power over others. This power sometimes has been economic and at other times political, but in either case the ability to control others' choices has caused enormous suffering. What sorts of institutions best fragment power and prevent some people from holding too much sway over the lives of others?

This question must be answered in the context of a realistic understanding of how the world operates. Whatever institutional arrangements exist, some people will be more powerful than others. The relevant issue is not what set of rules keeps people from having *any* control over others, but rather what institutions best limit the accumulation of power.

History is replete with examples of the misuse of coercive power in the hands of the State. One should therefore be suspicious of institutional arrangements that rely upon massive concentrations of power in the hands of the State, even though the explicit goal is to correct for injustices in the private economy. Societies without private property rights concentrate large amounts of power in the hands of a few, and that power traditionally has been badly abused.

A strong case can be made for an institutional order under which the state enforces clearly defined rules that keep people from imposing costs on others without their consent, but one in which the state is also limited in terms of the costs it can impose on individuals. A society where the government is responsible for defining and enforcing property rights, but where its role is also constitutionally limited, represents a viable combination. Such a system fragments power and restrains people from imposing costs on others without their consent.

Conclusion

A private property, market system has much to recommend it. A system is more moral if it holds individuals accountable for their actions and encourages them to help others than if it allows them to impose costs on others without their consent.

This is not to argue that a market system can serve as a replacement for a society in which people act on the basis of moral conscience. Individual morality certainly will enhance capitalism, as it would any system. Honesty, compassion, and empathy make our world more livable whatever the institutional arrangement. Capitalism is not inimical to these qualities. When alternative economic systems are evaluated within a moral framework, sound reasons emerge for favoring private property rights and markets. Markets and morality can serve as useful complements in maintaining a just society.

The Virtues of the Free Economy

by Bill Anderson

The minds of men are confused and muddled on the subject of economic freedom. The Western world in the last two centuries has been a showcase for the virtues of economic freedom, yet, as theologian Michael Novak points out, "Few themes are more common in Western intellectual history than the denigration of capitalism."[1] George Gilder, in his perceptive *Wealth and Poverty*, notes with sadness that many who give intellectual support to free enterprise do so not because they agree with its ethos (which they see as morally bankrupt), but simply for utilitarian reasons: it creates more wealth than does collectivism.[2]

Yet, if capitalism is to continue to be a vibrant part of the world order, it must be seen as having virtues beyond its immense productive capacities. Those who wish to enlist economic freedom in the quest for human progress, for justice, for an end to world hunger, for freedom itself, must see capitalism not only as an efficient dispensary for human greed, but basically as a conduit for moral actions. Capitalism is an economic way of life that can help promote not only material well-being, but also spiritual well-being.

At the present time, however, many people are abandoning the road to economic freedom and supporting, instead, the ethos of collectivism as they seek values they deem worthy. But such a road, Walter Lippmann wrote, "leads down to the abyss of tyranny, impoverishment and general war."[3] It is the purpose of this essay to examine this Western abandonment of capitalism and to show that the alternative to collectivism, the free economy, is, indeed, a worthy and moral choice by individuals and by nations.

The Paradox of Freedom

The free economy is a study in paradox. Persons vote against it at the polls and vote for it with their dollars. Collectivist govern-

---

Mr. Anderson is a doctoral student in economics at Auburn University. This article, which appeared in the April 1983 issue of *The Freeman*, is adapted from a prize-winning essay in the 1982 worldwide Olive W. Garvey Essay Competition, in association with the Mont Pelerin Society.

ments place it at the top of their enemies lists, yet turn to it to help cure their economic ills.[4] Clergymen denounce the capitalist spirit as immoral, yet the very foundation of the free market is dependent upon what Novak calls "the exercise of moral character of certain sorts."[5] The free market seems to have become a social prostitute: people of all income, education and cultural levels denounce it publicly for its alleged sins while at the same time seeking it in times of economic need.

Perhaps this is not surprising. After all, the intellectual and legal basis of capitalism—that the individual is free, has the ability (and responsibility) to make moral choices, and has certain rights that cannot be preempted by his government runs counter to the deeply held tenets of pantheistic traditional thought that have ruled human minds since the beginnings of civilization. At the heart of traditional thinking, whether it be articulated by a Plato, a Confucius, a Rousseau, a Castro, or a Mao, is the contention that one's identity begins not with himself but rather with his community, his guild, his tribe, his predetermined social class, or, in modern terms, his state.[6]

While it is true that Christianity (and especially the legacy of Protestantism) has undermined traditional thought—and gave spark to the rise of capitalism—the communal ideology of pantheism, with its emphasis on "aristocracy," social order, and varying rights and privileges to be granted to persons of different castes, became officially mixed with the Christian religion in the Middle Ages. Nor did the Protestant Reformation and its resulting doctrines instantly change the long-held conception of "superiors" and "inferiors" in the social order.[7]

The superiors included the clergy, the university professors, royalty, political figures and soldiers of high rank; the inferiors were the serfs, the merchants (who were especially distrusted) and other townspeople born of less than nobility. As one can imagine, such a "moral" order was more than popular with the upper classes, for along with being the natural heirs to leadership over the masses, they were free to impose their "superior" values upon their subjects, and that meant sumptuary laws and thousands of rules governing business practices.[8]

The historian Arthur M. Schlesinger, Jr., certainly showed an affinity for the pre-capitalist structures when he wrote of mercantilist England, "Power was held to imply responsibility, and all classes were to be brought together in harmonious union by a sense of reciprocal obligation."[9] Yet, as demonstrated by the numerous peasant uprisings that periodically threatened the foundation of the feudal order, it is clear that the masses did not share Schlesinger's enthusiasm for their plight. And well they did feel discontent; their lot was a most miserable one. The lower classes were as poverty-stricken then as the poorest villagers in destitute Third World nations today.

The vast number of regulations restricting price, supply, manufacturing procedures and—above all—competition, served as effective barriers to economic growth. Only the nobility could be wealthy; after all, believed the superiors, wealth was fixed and could only be divided, not expanded. It was unthinkable for one of a lesser social order to gain wealth. So when it came to gaining riches in the old world, "the worldly order," wrote Lippmann, "was to be predatory."[10] Neighbor plundered neighbor, city plundered city and nations constantly plundered nations.

It is of little wonder, then, that the aristocratic upper classes in post-mercantilist Europe neither appreciated nor understood the new capitalist economic and social revolution. After all, as one grasps when reading *The Wealth of Nations*, Adam Smith developed the concept of Natural Liberty precisely for the benefit of the poor, not the rich. The aristocrats could not comprehend the fact, as Lippmann put it, "that the Golden Rule was economically sound."[11] They could not envision the self-interest of the merchant being freely channeled to serve others, nor could they accept the merchant's gaining not only wealth but social prestige as well. The Industrial Revolution, in reality, was a revolution of the common man, and those who had once set the public agenda were left behind in democratic capitalism's wake.

And despite the vast increase of wealth and power capitalism has brought to the western world, and despite the great steps that have been made in eliminating the once common poverty in the industrial nations, the free market is still anathema to many of those outside the business realm—the New Class, as Irving Kristol calls them—who seek to determine the "social agenda." These people are hostile to business, but the reason for their hatred, in my opinion, has little to do with social and economic inequalities that exist within our society. After all, the traditional societies for which many of capitalism's critics share an affinity are often wretchedly poor with inequality the norm. As Kristol has noted, the reason for their contempt of the free market is the lack of social and political power the liberal, individualistic capitalistic order gives to them.[12] Within a society that permits a free market, power lies within the market itself, and "is dispersed among so much of [the] population rather than concentrated solely in a governing elite."[13]

Novak, commenting upon the hostility many clergymen seem to hold toward capitalism, writes:

> In traditional societies, church leaders (whether in Rome or in Geneva) were able to impose their own values on the entire civil society. It is difficult for church leaders to play such a role within a differentiated society. Thus there is often a secret hankering, a lingering nostalgia, for a planned society that would once again permit church leaders to be in alliance with civil leaders in suffusing an entire society with their values. This new Constantinianism appears today as socialism in totalitarian states, and as statism in mixed economies.[14]

Democracy in the Market

Critics of the capitalist system, especially those who might share the paternalistic biases of Kristol's "New Class," simply are not impressed with the democracy inherent within a market system. The aristocracy never had confidence in democratic institutions, especially during the pre-capitalist era; their descendants—though they may espouse a belief in democratic equality—have as little confidence in free choice as their forebears. For when they speak of equality, they talk not of a state of equality under law, but rather a state of equality *brought about* by the law. Their religion demands an equality of results to be administered by a governing elite.

Such a concept of law—that it restrain some and unleash others—is rooted not in the spirit of equality manifest by the rise of nineteenth-century liberalism, but rather in the despotic mentality of ancient tribalism. Therefore, the modern results of a legal system of equality by coercion—including progressive tax rates, transfer payments, housing subsidies, food stamps and other welfare programs, or the brutal results of twentieth-century collectivism reflect not some sort of advanced social compassion, but rather a mental leap backward into an age of monarchs who thought themselves chosen to rule by divine fiat.[15] And such a mentality, it needs to be stressed, mutually excludes the liberal view of equality before the law. For where inequality before the law prevails, so prevails the specter of despotism, of tyranny, of poverty, and loss of personal freedom.

Henry Hazlitt, Gilder, Kristol, and others have intelligently argued that government poverty programs based on legal inequality actually retard potential economic gains poor persons can make. What they have not pointed out, however, is the link between today's agenda of statism and the paternalistic ethos of ancient times. And it is here that nations can learn from the past, for it is the indisputable fact of history that legal inequality, enforced economic isolation (called self-sufficiency) and the throttling of the free market leads not to the desired ends of justice and prosperity, but to the reverse. It has only been the practice of free division of labor, free markets, and equality before the law that has led to freedom and economic growth. It has long been the contention of traditional man that he must choose between liberty and bread; the experience of freedom has demonstrated the opposite. Liberty leads to more bread, and much else besides.

Ultimately, it is both the liberty and prosperity inherent in the democratic capitalist order that brings those grounded in ancient ideals of society to a distrust of the free market. For the liberty of this order permits those who once labored under the domination of despots to govern themselves, while the prosperity brought about by the free market system allows those who once were desperately poor to support themselves and not be dependent upon the paternalistic whims of the aristocracy. Lippmann once commented about those who seek, in effect, the older order:

> . . . the only instrument of progress in which they have faith is the coercive agency of government. They can imagine no alternative, nor can they remember how much of what they cherish as progressive has come by emancipation from political dominion, by the limitation of power, by the release of personal energy from authority and collective coercion.[16]

And it was Frederic Bastiat who so eloquently predicted the

results in store for those who seek coercion under the guise of freedom:

> Capital, under the impact of such a doctrine, will hide, flee, be destroyed. And what will become, then, of the workers, those workers for whom you profess an affection so deep and sincere but so unenlightened? Will they be better fed when agricultural production is stopped? Will they be better dressed when no one dares build a factory? Will they have more employment when capital will have disappeared?[17]

Giving and Receiving

One who gives is held in far greater esteem than one who receives, and it is widely believed by those embracing traditional views that capitalism is simply the economy of receiving, that is, the poor labor and the rich receive. Hence the view, articulated by John C. Bennett, president emeritus of Union Theological Seminary, that the free economy, if not altered by forces of government, is "morally intolerable."[18]

Economic freedom as demonstrated by two centuries of unparalleled fiscal growth, has given those nations that practice it wealth that far exceeds even the richest monarchies of ancient times. And yet, the spirit of economic freedom is seen by critics as just "the unguided lust of the businessman for profit."[19] Schlesinger, an outspoken advocate of the planned economy, describes the philosophy of free enterprise as an anarchic creed of "everyone for himself and the devil take the hindmost."[20] And Ronald J . Sider, author of *Rich Christians in an Age of Hunger*, dismisses capitalistic economic growth as simply the product of covetousness.

> One cannot read the parable of the rich fool [in the New Testament] without thinking of our own society. We madly multiply more sophisticated gadgets, larger and taller buildings and faster means of transportation not because such things truly enrich our lives but because we are driven by an obsession for more and more. Covetousness—a striving for more and more material possessions—has become a cardinal vice of Western civilization.[21]

Such charges—and they are legion—bring one to ask obvious

questions, and they are: Have the vast improvements in the material quality of life, life-saving drugs, mass education, the elimination of famine, the breaking down of structures that once enslaved persons of little means, and the concept of individual liberty arisen simply from greed, from covetousness, from the desire to harm one's neighbor? Have the economic gains made in the past two hundred years by the descendants of those once legally bound as serfs been simply a moral blight on history?

I leave the reader of this essay to answer those questions for himself. But my point is this: Capitalism has brought vast economic improvements to nations practicing it; that is not in dispute. However, if the free market order is seen by a majority of men—and especially those who have the power to set social agendas—as a license for greed, decadence, and moral bankruptcy, then nations will continue their slide toward collectivism and statism and what is left of the free market will disappear into the dishonesty, graft, and bribery that is the black market.[22]

In establishing moral criteria for judging capitalism, I believe the free market must pass two tests. First, it must be consistent with the principles of the time-honored Golden Rule; second, the society that produces the capitalist system must be a moral one that measures up to certain moral principles.

Living by the Golden Rule

In a predatory economy, the Golden Rule, "Do unto others as you would have them do unto you," cannot be practiced easily. If wealth can be gained only by extraction, then it seems logical to assume that one cannot become rich and simultaneously live by the Golden Rule. Either one steals (and no one likes to be called a thief) or one is poor (which demonstrates why poverty has been held in such esteem in traditional religious thought). Traditional thinking dictates that a society governed by the Golden Rule be poor; it is not difficult to understand, then, why a mind governed by such ideas would interpret the capitalist society as rapacious.

But, as Lippmann, Mises, Gilder, and others have articulated, the prosperity of the free market order has developed not as the result of theft, but rather by the forces of mutual cooperation and trust between individuals. Lippmann's thesis of *The Good Society* was that a moral, cooperative society could come about *only* by the practice of free market principles. He wrote:

> All of this [Western prosperity] did not happen by some sort of spontaneous enlightenment and upsurge of good will. The characters of men were not suddenly altered. . . . For the first time in human history men had come upon a way of producing wealth in which the good fortune of others multiplied their own. It was a great moment, for example, in the long history of conquest, rapine, and oppression when David Hume could say (1742) . . . "I shall therefore venture to acknowledge, that, not only as a man, but as a British subject, I pray for the flourishing commerce of Germany, Spain, Italy, and even France itself." It had not occurred to many men before that the Golden Rule was economically sound.[23]

For one to gain wealth in the capitalistic system, notes Gilder, one must first *give*, not receive. "The gifts of advanced capitalism in a monetary economy are called investments. . . . The gifts will succeed only to the extent that they are altruistic and spring from an understanding of the needs of others."[24] Wrote Mises:

> Wealth can be acquired only by serving the consumers. The capitalists lose their funds as soon as they fail to invest them in those lines in which they satisfy best the demands of the public.[25]

Within such a system of freedom, one is rewarded only if his neighbor is also rewarded. "A" profits only when voluntary choice prevails—by giving "B" either a product or a service which "B" feels will meet his needs or desires.[26] If this interaction were to cease, the intricate web of cooperation that supports the capitalist system would quickly break down. Retailers would not sell if they could not trust their producers; consumers would not buy if they had no confidence in the products and services available. Investment would not be possible if those with the means to save and invest had neither confidence in nor concern for the future.

As demonstrated by Leonard Read in his 1958 article "I, Pencil," even the basic products made within the capitalist system involve the cooperation of thousands of persons, even persons who by sight or creed might hate each other. Such is the power of the free market. It is no coincidence, then, as Hans Sennholz points out, that the capitalist nineteenth century—so condemned by its critics as a hundred years of exploitation—was the most peaceful century in human history.[27]

The Moral Foundations

When Adam Smith in 1776 laid out his thesis in *The Wealth of Nations*, he envisioned the free market order to arise not from a people controlled by avarice, greed, and ill-will, but rather from a society in which moral values were considered to be important, where creativity, sympathy, thrift, and the postponing of present gratification for future reward were upheld as virtuous. Such an order had already arisen in Puritan New England, where the virtues so vital to the establishment of a growing free market had become the basis of the region that gave birth to Yankee Ingenuity.

> Puritanism gave the pursuit of such interests (work, thrift and enterprise) divine sanction and showed that this working of divine will through an individual's daily work could be advantageous to society at large. . . . It was because the Puritan . . . was satisfied to postpone or delay his gratification, that capital accumulation was made possible and that investment leading to new kinds of productivity emerged.[28]

Conversely, one might add, the societies which are predatory and show little of the moral virtues as have been described, are also societies that show little or no economic promise. For as Novak has so eloquently stated, capitalism is not the end result of materialism. Rather, materialism—that is, the insatiable desire for instant material gratification—works against the free market. He notes:

> Sustained economic growth does not consist solely in material abundance; it springs from and it continues to demand the exercise of moral character of certain sorts. Should such character disappear, so would sustained economic growth. A hedonistic, narcissistic culture is not likely to invest in its own future or to make the necessary sacrifices for its own posterity.[29]

Outstanding Economic Growth a Consequence of Freedom

Despite the fact that breathtaking economic growth has occurred for more than 200 years, those two centuries, when placed in the context of the millennia of human history, are but a blink of an eye. The rise in the living standards of men once destined to live in squalor and oppression has come perhaps too quickly for most who have participated in or have been caught up in the capitalist order. Men have profited greatly from the free economy, but few have ever understood why this sudden increase in prosperity even occurred. Thus, men, who are inclined to follow the traditional philosophies so firmly etched in their minds, easily fall prey to those who would offer them coercion and collectivism as the road to an even better life.

But the genie of freedom has been allowed to escape, and men, even while not understanding fully how freedom has given them economic opportunity, still have tasted of its fruits. Because of the phenomenon of individual freedom, the shackles that bound the serfs—and even their oppressive monarchs—in the precapitalist era have, at least, been discarded temporarily. Therefore, men can dream of a better life where their ancestors could only accept the poverty of their day.

The experience of the free economy leaves one both optimistic and pessimistic at the same time. One is optimistic, because it has been demonstrated for 200 years that freedom works, brings a better life to all, and is not a force to be feared. But one is also pessimistic, because so many have failed to understand the virtues of the free economy and, therefore, turn to collectivism and statism in hopes that coercion will allow them to fulfill their dreams.

The free economy allows men to be virtuous, to practice trust and honesty and be rewarded for it, to provide a good life for their fellows, to help rid the world of plagues, hunger and other blights that prey upon the weakest of those in our midst. It promotes cooperation instead of conflict; it encourages peace instead of war.

When Lippmann exhorted his peers to turn from the drive to statism in the 1930s, he was jeered and declared by many of his fellow "liberals" to be a "reactionary." And, yet, many of his insights were correct, many of his predictions of coming wars accurate. They are true today as well.

The message of Lippmann, and the message 200 years of liberty has proclaimed is this: the Good Society, one in which men can strive for justice, virtue and a better life for all can come about only by the practice which "preserves and strives to perfect the freedom of the market."[30]

This is not a utopian dream, for those who believe in utopia believe also that man can be coerced into perfection. I cannot accept the idea that somehow man in the world as we know it will lose his willingness to sin. But while man is in his imperfect state, the free economy will help him to create a more prosperous, a more tolerant, a more just, and a more virtuous world.

---

1. Michael Novak, "The Economic System: The Evangelical Basis for a Social Market Economy," *The Review of Politics*, July 1981, Vol. 43, p. 355.
2. George Gilder, *Wealth and Poverty* (New York: Basic Books, 1981), p. 4.
3. Walter Lippmann, *The Good Society* (Boston: Little, Brown, 1937), p. 204.
4. Lenin's New Economic Policy of 1923, Stalin's introduction of differential wages, and other "capitalist" practices in 1931, and the encouragement of small, private enterprises in present-day Communist China are notable examples of despotic, collectivist governments seeking help from the free market.
5. Novak, p. 365.
6. J. Kautz expressed the traditionalist ideals in his 1860 work *Die geschichtliche Entwickelung der Nationökonomik* when he described the pantheistic views of Hindu India. "Above all," wrote Kautz, "as a controlling fundamental of the entire social and economic theory of India can be placed the esthetics self-denial and renunciation, the unreserved recognition and glorification of absolute political despotism, the denial of the personal worth of man."
7. The Calvinistic *Westminster Confession of Faith*, composed 1643–1648, deals with the Fifth Commandment (Honor your father and mother) by extending the concept of parents to include social "superiors" as well.
8. For example, during the French monarchy from 1666 until 1730 the French textile industry faced a mountain of regulations contained in four quarto volumes of 2,200 pages and three supplementary volumes.
9. Arthur M. Schlesinger, Jr., "Neo-Conservatism and the Class Struggle," the *Wall Street Journal*, June 2, 1981, p. 30.
10. Lippmann, p. 194.
11. *Ibid.*
12. Irving Kristol, *Two Cheers for Capitalism* (New York: Basic Books, 1978), p. 28.
13. Robert Heilbroner, "Is Capitalism Working?", *Time*, April 21, 1980. Heilbroner is an advocate of the planned society.
14. Michael Novak, *Toward a Theology of Cooperation* (Washington, D.C.: American Enterprise Institute, 1981), pp. 11–12.
15. See "Inside North Korea, Marxism's First 'Monarchy,'" *Reader's Digest*, February 1982.
16. Lippmann, p. 5.
17. Quoted in William H. Peterson, "Creating a 'Negative-Sum' Society," *Business Week*, November 16, 1981, p. 32.
18. John C. Bennett, "Reaganethics," *Christianity and Crisis*, December 14, 1981, p. 339.
19. "The New Deal in Review, 1936-1940," *The New Republic*, May 20, 1940, p. 707.
20. Schlesinger, p. 30.
21. Ronald J. Sider, *Rich Christians in an Age of Hunger* (Downers Grove, Ill.: Inter-Varsity Press, 1977), p. 123.
22. For in-depth looks into how a state strangled economy invites black-market activity, read Antonio Martino, "Measuring Italy's Underground Economy," *Policy Review*,

Spring 1981, and Ken Adelman's description of black-market corruption in socialist Tanzania in "The Great Black Hope," *Harper's*, July 1981.

23. Lippmann, pp. 193–4.

24. Gilder, pp. 24, 27.

25. Ludwig von Mises, *The Anti-Capitalistic Mentality* (South Holland, Ill.: Libertarian Press, 1972), p. 2.

26. In a planned society where the State makes economic choices for its citizens, people must "choose," then, whatever the State gives them. Under these conditions, however, the products and services usually leave much to be desired and the result is a bullied, dissatisfied customer.

27. Hans F. Sennholz, "Welfare States at War," *The Freeman*, January 1981.

28. James T. Laney, "The Other Adam Smith," *Economic Review*, October 1981, p. 28.

29. Novak, "The Economic System: The Evangelical Basis of a Social Market Economy," pp. 365–366.

30. Lippmann, p. 207.

On Private Property and Economic Power

by Hans F. Sennholz

In their denunciation of our social order the socialists usually follow two patterns of attack. While some depict in glowing colors the desirability of socialism, others describe the alleged horrors of the individual enterprise system. In his *Moral Man and Immoral Society* Reinhold Niebuhr mainly adheres to the latter while pleading the casc for socialism. This book virtually "made" Niebuhr when it appeared in 1934. It provides the lenses through which many people, even today, view social problems.

We agree with Niebuhr that power is evil and ought to be distrusted. But "only the Marxian proletarian," says Niebuhr, "has seen this problem with perfect clarity. If he makes mistakes in choosing the means of accomplishing his ends, he has made no mistake either in stating the rational goal toward which society must move, the goal of equal justice, or in understanding the economic foundations of justice." (pp. 164–165) Only the Marxian proletarian has recognized this.

When Niebuhr speaks of the "ruling classes,"—by which he means the defenders of capitalism—he uses harsh terms such as "prejudice," "hypocrisy," and "dishonesty." Their reasoning, religion, and culture, according to Niebuhr, "are themselves the product of, or at least colored by, the partial experience of the class." (pp. 140–141) In other words, anyone defending individual freedom, private property, and enterprise, is unmasked as an advocate of the special privileges and interests of the bourgeois class.

According to Niebuhrian philosophy the population is divided into economic classes whose interests differ radically from each other. But only the Marxian proletarian strives at rational goals toward which a just society must move. The individual enterprise order is corrupt and unjust because it is built on the special interests and economic powers of the bourgeois class.

Dr. Sennholz was chairman of the economics department at Grove City College, Pennsylvania, for thirty-seven years. Author of several books and hundreds of articles, he is now the president of FEE. This article originally appeared in the January 1961 issue of *The Freeman*.

All three suppositions are fallacious. There are no classes, no class privileges in the society contemplated by the classic philosophers and economists. Before the law everyone is to be treated equally. The ancient privileges of rank, estate, or class were abolished by repeal legislation during the eighteenth and nineteenth centuries.

Private Wealth Consists of Capital

Private property is no special privilege enjoyed by the bourgeois class. It is a natural institution that facilitates orderly production and division of labor. Private ownership of the means of production is in the interest of everyone, for it assures the most economic employment of scarce resources. The efficient entrepreneur, who produces what the people want in the most efficient manner, acquires control over productive capital. His wealth mainly consists of capital employed in the production of goods for the people.

The critics of capitalism who deplore the great differences between the wealthy industrialist and workingmen overlook this characteristic of the industrialist's wealth. His wealth does not consist of idle luxuries, but of factories, machines, and equipment that produce for the people, provide employment, and yield high wages. It is true the successful entrepreneur usually enjoys a higher standard of living than his employee. The car he drives may be a later model. The suit he wears may be custom-made and his house may have wall-to-wall carpeting. But his living conditions do not differ essentially from those of his workers.

Economic Power Is Derivative

The businessman's power is derived from the sovereign power to consumers. His ability to manage wisely the factors of production earns him the consumer's support. This is not anchored in legal privilege, custom, or tradition, but in his ability to serve the only sovereign boss of the capitalist economy: the consumer. The businessman, no matter how great his powers may appear, must cater to the whims and wishes of the buyers. To neglect them spells disaster to him.

A well-known example may illustrate the case. Henry Ford rose to fame, wealth, and power when he produced millions of cars that people liked and desired. But during the late 1920s their tastes and preferences began to change. They wanted a greater variety of bigger and better cars which Ford refused to manufacture. Consequently, while other companies such as General Motors and Chrysler grew by leaps and bounds, the Ford enterprise suffered staggering losses. Thus the power and reputation of Henry Ford declined, for a time, as rapidly as it had grown during the earlier decades.

It is true that a businessman probably can afford to disregard or disappoint a single buyer. But he must pay the price in the form of lower sales and earnings. If he continuously disappoints his buyers, he will soon be eliminated from the rank of entrepreneurs.

It is also true that a businessman may be rude and unfair toward an employee. But he must pay a high price for his arbitrariness. His men tend to leave him and seek employment with competitors. In order to attract the needed labor, the businessman in ill repute will have to pay a premium above the wages paid by more considerate competitors. But higher costs lead to his elimination. If he pays lower wages, he loses his efficient help to his competitors, which, too, entails his elimination.

A successful businessman is dependable, reliable, and fair. He endeavors to earn the trust and goodwill of his customers as well as of his workers. In fact, the businessman's striving for goodwill may shape a colorless personality. In order to avoid controversy and hostility, he mostly withholds or even refrains from forming an opinion on political or economic issues. Many businessmen aim to be neutral with regard to all controversial problems and issues.

Capitalism a Haven for Workingman

A capitalist society is a haven for workingmen who are the greatest beneficiaries of its order. One merely needs to compare the working and living conditions of the American worker with those of his colleagues in noncapitalistic countries, such as India or China. He is the prince among the world's laborers; his work week is the shortest, his physical exertion the least, and his wages are by far the highest.

The millionaire is less enviable in capitalism than in noncapitalist societies. His wealth mainly consists of capital investments which he must defend continuously in keen competition with other businessmen. His consumptive wealth, which is a minor fraction of his total wealth, probably is rather modest. But the Indian millionaire, most likely a rajah, is not concerned with production and competition. He resides in a huge mansion, surrounded by his harem and catered to by dozens of eager servants. He certainly does not envy the American industrialist, however great the latter's wealth may be.

Socialism, whether of Marxian, Fabian, Nazi, or Fascist brand, does not promote equality, but instead creates tremendous inequalities. It gives rise to a new class of political and economic administrators whose powers of economic management are unlimited and absolute. It eliminates the sovereign power of consumers and the agency powers of businessmen. It substitutes omniscient rulers and an omnipotent state for the people's freedom of choice and discretion.

It may be true that the Marxian worker actually strives for the realization of such a society; but contrary to Niebuhr's beliefs, his endeavors certainly benefit neither society nor himself. Blinded and misguided by socialist syllogisms, he promotes a social order that will enslave and impoverish him. Thus he destroys the very order that has freed him from serfdom and starvation.

Capitalism Is Merciless—to Capitalists

by Allan Levite

Attending college in the late 1960s left me with many unique memories. Among these was the economics class in which the instructor told the students that such firms as IBM and Xerox were so huge and powerful that they dominated their markets. Smaller competitors were helpless against them. They exercised such tremendous control over patents and technology, and spent so much on research and development, that other firms in their industries could never hope to compete effectively, much less overtake them. For these reasons, government intervention was necessary to protect both consumers and competitors.

Of course, this sort of thinking was neither confined to the 1960s nor the exclusive product of economics professors. Many decades ago, socialist author George Orwell, in an effort to demonstrate the superiority of socialism over capitalism, made much the same point when he mentioned a phonograph company that had bought a patent for a superior phonograph needle. The company did not produce the needle and never intended to. It simply wanted to kill the invention, so that it would not compete with its existing product line. (Orwell seems to have forgotten that patents are government-created and government-enforced monopolies.) He used this example to illustrate his point that capitalism suppresses more technology than it creates. Under capitalism, he wrote, money is risked only on projects that promise quick profits. Remove the profit principle, he claimed, and inventors would have a free hand.[1]

But time has completely disproven his theory. The phonograph companies were completely unable to use this tactic or any other to stop the spread of cassette tape and CD-ROM technology. This is an ample illustration that no matter how much they might try, capitalists cannot repeal the laws of markets. (Governments have also tried to do so, with the same lack of success.) For brief peri-

---

Mr. Levite is a free-lance writer residing in San Francisco, California. This article originally appeared in the June 1995 issue of *The Freeman*.

ods, capitalists can dominate markets or industries, but the achievement of such domination is always temporary. It sets in motion forces that no capitalist or group of capitalists could ever control. Lucrative profits, for example, attract competitors; and soon, the level of profit evens out. This does not prove Marx's thesis about the falling rate of profit, for a decline of profitability in one industry will be offset by gains in another. But it does help to disprove the notion that "the big boys" run things. If they did, they would surely be able to prevent the loss of their own markets!

Both IBM and Xerox had ample power over technology by means of their tremendous research expenditures and control of patents, but it did not help them keep their markets. As for projects presumably being squelched because they do not offer quick profits, one need only compare the number of new ventures that appeared in socialist countries with the number that appear in capitalist countries. Whether or not a project promises profits is largely a matter of guesswork—that is, opinion. And opinions are never lacking. The mere fact that so many profit-oriented ventures fail is sufficient proof that a venture hardly needs to be demonstrably lucrative to be attempted.

On occasion, a product will enjoy such success among consumers that its leadership over competitive brands will appear to be unassailable. Backed by the profits thus generated, the firm will spend large sums on advertising to maintain the product's leadership. Competitors will be unable to supplant it. Because of this market domination, the lucky corporation is protected from price competition and can unfairly maintain monopoly prices and profits—or so we are told. This certainly seemed to be the case with Marlboro cigarettes, which has been the leading brand for a long time. I've never smoked myself, so I've always wondered if Marlboro's market leadership was solely the product of its hugely successful advertising efforts. But most of the smokers I've asked believe that Marlboros taste better than other brands. Despite this presumably better taste, however, and even though Philip Morris spends enormous sums on advertising this brand, it has lost some of its market share to low-priced "generic" cigarettes, which are hardly even advertised. Philip Morris was forced to respond by lowering Marlboro's price by 40 cents per pack, which increased its market share by about 5 percent, but contributed to a fall in the company's operating profit from $5.2 billion to $2.8 billion.[2] There have been very few instances in business history of brands as successful and powerful as Marlboro. Yet it could still not resist these competitive pressures.

Price Competition in the Computer Industry

The necessity of competing in terms of price is nothing new, nor is it confined to cigarettes. The company I work for sells hard disks for personal computers. The extent to which prices of PC's have dropped in the last ten years is already well known, but let me provide a typical example from our price lists. Our Fall 1991 price list showed a price of $5,099 for a 1-gigabyte (1,000-megabyte) SCSI hard disk. The current [1995] price for a drive of that capacity is $1,099—a drop of $4,000. Not only that, but our newer model also takes up less desk space and transfers data at a 42 percent faster rate.

Such examples did not need to wait for the development of the PC. Penicillin sold at first for $20 per dose. As more and more companies began to manufacture it, the price eventually dropped to 2 cents.[3] In 1908, Henry Ford's Model-T Touring Car sold for $850. Eight years later, a new Ford Touring Car sold for only $360.[4] A labor union would consider it a great victory to have won for its members as much money as these capitalists allowed consumers to save. If a government bureau had disbursed the same amounts to the public, high school history textbooks from that era to this one would have been praising the foresight and benevolence of the bureau's policies.

If capitalists had as much control over markets and prices as we have been led to believe, it seems highly unlikely that they would permit such price drops to occur. If costs decline, why not just maintain the retail price at its previous level and reap huge profits? The answer is that this cannot be done. Even the less astute capitalists are quick to see that if they drop prices just a little, additional sales can be gathered. Naturally, as Adam Smith pointed out over two centuries ago, they would also be quick to see that it would be advantageous to conspire together and agree to fix prices at certain levels, preventing a price war. But such agreements never last long. The same economic forces that inspire capitalists to make such pacts also break the pacts apart. Even if outsiders who are not parties to the agreement can somehow be kept under control and prevented from undercutting prices, the parties to the agreement will not hold to it for long. There is always more to be gained from breaking the covenant than from sticking to it. More importantly, consumers will find substitutes for the price-fixed product if they perceive that its price is being held above the true market price, which reflects the value they put on it.

The most noteworthy point about the conspiratorial argument is that anyone who accepts it would have to assume that *all* capitalists would operate in this manner. To be sure, all capitalists are driven by the prospect of financial gain, so they would all have a strong incentive to keep profits high by fixing prices and avoiding price competition. Geographic distance would no longer minimize this effect. It is true that foreign trade has played an increasingly important role in the world economy, and that capitalists in one country now compete against capitalists in other countries. But if capitalists in different countries wish to conspire together to fix prices, modern means of communication make this no more difficult than placing a phone call.

The capitalists in the computer industry would be characterized by all this no less than any others. But as we have seen, price wars have been the rule nevertheless, and not only in any one country, but on a worldwide basis. This gives us an excellent opportunity to look back in retrospect on the Justice Department's antitrust suit against IBM, which was riddled with inaccuracies and contradictions, and which had to keep changing its premises to keep pace with changes in the market. In 1982, the Solicitor General finally decided that the case was without merit and dropped it—after both sides had wasted hundreds of millions of dollars fighting it.[5] (Part of this was money that IBM might have spent on research and development.) But if the government had wanted to break up IBM, it could have done so without spending a penny of taxpayers' money. It could simply have waited for the market to do the job. In 1993, IBM lost eight *billion* dollars.

The Pitfalls of Bureaucratic Management

This illustrates that the market is not the only force that tends to cut giant firms down to size. Technology and bureaucracy can do that all by themselves. IBM has been the victim of both. Computer technology has made mainframe computers—IBM's mainstay—increasingly obsolete. IBM could have shifted entirely to smaller machines, but its bureaucracy resisted change for too long. Bureaucracy not only displaces the entrepreneurial spirit that turns small firms into big ones, it also makes the entrepreneurial spirit unwelcome. Big firms become bureaucratic, and bureaucratic firms become cumbersome and slow to respond to customers' needs. Decisions take too long to make, and smaller firms that are not encumbered by such problems find ways to serve customers' needs better. Government bureaucracies can endure because governments do not need to make a profit or to respond to competitive pressures. But in industry, the bureaucracy that is typical in large firms can undermine the most powerful corporations and gradually decrease their market power, while increasing that of the smaller firms.

This is not to say that IBM was inefficient or that it produced bad products. In fact, it has always been known for making good products, which is why it got to be as big as it was. But even good products cannot create and hold monopolies, because substitutes exist and because even firms that make good products might not be making the *right* products for the market. Despite IBM's size and strength, other firms began to make other products that many of IBM's customers started using as substitutes for IBM's mainframes. The market "grew up," and no longer wished to be as dependent on IBM and its machines as it had been. The advent of PC's made it possible for customers to write or buy software that could perform the tasks they needed done, without depending on IBM.

Socialism and Innovation

But couldn't socialism accomplish the same thing, by simply breaking up large corporations or nationalizing them? Let's analyze how this would work—specifically, how it would treat innovations, since economic growth depends on innovations. Suppose that the government had taken over all industry by 1970. In 1975, a government planning bureau would have been visited by Steve Jobs and Steve Wozniak, the founders of Apple Computer. These young hobbyists would have had to ask the bureau to allocate funds for their project. But the government bureau would have had little reason to redirect money that had been destined to fill immediate needs, and devote it instead to an untried, unproven, and highly doubtful project—one that had nothing to do with necessities such as food, shelter, and health care. To top it all off, Jobs and Wozniak were neither recognized authorities nor successful managers. Worse still, in order for their machine to be useful, someone would have had to write software programs for it, which had not been done at that time. But in a country where the profit motive existed, the "two Steves" had little difficulty finding venture capitalists willing to fund their project. The fact that IBM dominated the computer industry at the time did not retard their progress in the least.

Many *unanticipated* uses were found for the machine they created. Socialist planning does not take unanticipated uses into account, and couldn't even if it wanted to. The trial-and-error system of profit and loss determines what works much more adequately than central planning ever could. And if the project of the "two Steves" had failed (under capitalism), only the venture capitalists would have suffered a financial loss. Under socialism, the taxpayers as a whole would have borne the loss. *This* is why Orwell's fears that capitalism would suppress innovation are groundless, although they would be true with respect to socialism.

What lessons can we draw from all this? First of all, capitalism is a great force for efficiency. It rewards firms that serve their customers' needs and punishes firms that are inefficient. It allows firms to grow to huge size and to amass great wealth—if they earn it. If they cease to do so, or if competitors do it better, they will decline, no matter how big and powerful they were.

These are lessons we should all ponder the next time we are told that the powers of the government must be enlisted to redirect industrial activity towards various "public" goals.

---

1. George Orwell, *The Road to Wigan Pier* (New York: Harcourt Brace Jovanovich, 1958), pp. 206–07.
2. Andrew E. Server, "How to Escape a Price War," *Fortune*, June 13, 1994, p. 83.
3. Stanley Siegelman, "Pharmaceuticals," *Chemical Week*, August 2, 1989, p. 32.
4. Richard S. Tedlow, *New and Improved: The Story of Mass Marketing in America* (New York: Basic Books, 1990), p. 125.
5. Charles H. Ferguson and Charles R. Morris, *Computer Wars* (New York: Times Books, 1994), pp. 10–11.

IV. THE ANTI-CAPITALIST MENTALITY

Socialism

by Ludwig von Mises

I am in Buenos Aires as a guest of the Centro de Difusión de la Economía Libre. What is *economía libre*? What does this system of economic freedom mean? The answer is simple: it is the market economy, it is the system in which the cooperation of individuals in the social division of labor is achieved by the market. This market is not a place; it is *a process*, it is the way in which, by selling and buying, by producing and consuming, the individuals contribute to the total workings of society.

In dealing with this system of economic organization—the market economy—we employ the term "economic freedom." Very often, people misunderstand what it means, believing that economic freedom is something quite apart from other freedoms and that these other freedoms—which they hold to be more important—can be preserved even in the absence of economic freedom. The meaning of economic freedom is this: that the individual is in a position to *choose* the way in which he wants to integrate himself into the totality of society. The individual is able to choose his career, he is free to do what he *wants* to do.

This is of course not meant in the sense which so many people attach to the word freedom today; it is meant rather in the sense that, through economic freedom, man is freed from natural conditions. In nature, there is nothing that can be termed freedom, there is only the regularity of the laws of nature, which man must obey if he wants to attain something.

In using the term freedom as applied to human beings, we think only of freedom *within society*. Yet, today, social freedoms are considered by many people to be independent of one another. Those who call themselves "liberals" today are asking for policies which are precisely the opposite of those policies which the liberals of the

---

Dr. Ludwig von Mises (1881–1973) was dean of the Austrian school of economics and a guiding light for FEE during its early years. Mises was far ahead of his time, and the lessons of his many books—especially *Socialism* and *Human Action*—are still growing in impact.

This article, which appeared in the January 1980 issue of *The Freeman*, is adapted from a chapter in his book *Economic Policy: Thoughts for Today and Tomorrow*.

nineteenth century advocated in their liberal programs. The so-called liberals of today have the very popular idea that freedom of speech, of thought, of the press, freedom of religion, freedom from imprisonment without trial—that all these freedoms can be preserved in the absence of what is called economic freedom. They do not realize that, in a system where there is no market, where the government directs everything, all those other freedoms are illusory, even if they are made into laws and written up in constitutions.

Let us take one freedom, the freedom of the press. If the government owns all the printing presses, it will determine what is to be printed and what is not to be printed. And if the government owns all the printing presses and determines what shall or shall not be printed, then the possibility of printing any kind of opposing arguments against the ideas of the government becomes practically nonexistent. Freedom of the press disappears. And it is the same with all the other freedoms.

Freedom in Society

In a market economy, the individual has the freedom to choose whatever career he wishes to pursue, to choose his own way of integrating himself into society. But in a socialist system, that is not so: his career is decided by decree of the government. The government can order people whom it dislikes, whom it does not want to live in certain regions, to move into other regions and to other places. And the government is always in a position to justify and to explain such procedure by declaring that the governmental plan requires the presence of this eminent citizen five thousand miles away from the place in which he could be disagreeable to those in power.

It is true that the freedom a man may have in a market economy is not perfect freedom from the metaphysical point of view. But there is no such thing as perfect freedom. Freedom means something only within the framework of society. The eighteenth-century authors of "natural law"—above all, Jean Jacques Rousseau—believed that once, in the remote past, men enjoyed something called "natural" freedom. But in that remote age, individuals were not free, they were at the mercy of everyone who was stronger than they were. The famous words of Rousseau: "Man is born free and everywhere he is in chains" may sound good, but man is in fact *not* born free. Man is born a very weak suckling. Without the protection of his parents, without the protection given to his parents by society, he would not be able to preserve his life.

Freedom in society means that a man depends as much upon other people as other people depend upon him. Society under the market economy, under the conditions of *economía libre*, means a state of affairs in which everybody serves his fellow citizens and is served by them in return. People believe that there are in the market economy bosses who are independent of the good will and support of other people. They believe that the captains of industry, the businessmen, the entrepreneurs are the real bosses in the economic system. But this is an illusion. The real bosses in the economic system are the consumers. And if the consumers stop patronizing a branch of business, these businessmen are either forced to abandon their eminent position in the economic system or to adjust their actions to the wishes and to the orders of the consumers.

One of the best-known propagators of communism was Lady Passfield, known under her maiden name, Beatrice Potter, and also known in collaboration with her husband, Sidney Webb. This lady was the daughter of a wealthy businessman and, when she was a young adult, she served as her father's secretary. In her memoirs she writes: "In the business of my father everybody had to obey the orders issued by my father, the boss. He alone had to give orders, but to him nobody gave any orders." This is a very shortsighted view. Orders *were* given to her father by the consumers, by the buyers. Unfortunately, she could not see *these* orders; she could not see what goes on in a market economy, because she was interested only in the orders given within her father's office or his factory.

Sovereign Consumers

In all economic problems, we must bear in mind the words of the great French economist Frederic Bastiat, who titled one of his brilliant essays: *"Ce qu'on voit et ce qu'on ne voit pas"* ("That which is seen and that which is not seen"). In order to comprehend the operation of an economic system, we must deal not only with the things that can be seen, but we also have to give our attention to the things which cannot be perceived directly. For instance, an order issued by a boss to an office boy can be heard by everybody who is present in the room. What cannot be heard are the orders given to the boss by his customers.

The fact is that, under the capitalistic system, the ultimate bosses are the consumers. The sovereign is not the state, it is the people. And the proof that they are the sovereign is borne out by the fact that they have *the right to be foolish*. This is the privilege of the sovereign. He has the right to make mistakes, no one can prevent him from making them, but of course he has to pay for his mistakes. If we say the consumer is supreme or that the consumer is sovereign, we do not say that the consumer is free from faults, that the consumer is a man who always knows what would be best for him. The consumers very often buy things or consume things they ought not to buy or ought not to consume.

But the notion that a capitalist form of government can prevent people from hurting themselves by controlling their consumption is false. The idea of government as a paternal authority, as a guardian for everybody, is the idea of those who favor socialism. In the United States some years ago, the government tried what was called "a noble experiment." This noble experiment was a law making it illegal to consume intoxicating beverages. It is certainly true that many people drink too much brandy and whiskey, and that they may hurt themselves by doing so. Some authorities in the United States are even opposed to smoking. Certainly there are many people who smoke too much and who smoke in spite of the fact that it would be better for them not to smoke. This raises a question which goes far beyond economic discussion: it shows what freedom really means.

Granted, that it is good to keep people from hurting themselves by drinking or smoking too much. But once you have admitted this, other people will say: Is the body everything? Is not the mind of man much more important? Is not the mind of man the real human endowment, the real human quality? If you give the government the right to determine the consumption of the human body, to determine whether one should smoke or not smoke, drink or not drink, there is no good reply you can give to people who say: "More important than the body is the mind and the soul, and man hurts himself much more by reading bad books, by listening to bad music and looking at bad movies. Therefore it is the duty of the government to prevent people from committing these faults."

And, as you know, for many hundreds of years governments and authorities believed that this really was their duty. Nor did this happen in far distant ages only; not long ago, there was a government in Germany that considered it a governmental duty to distinguish between good and bad paintings—which of course meant good and bad from the point of view of a man who, in his youth, had failed the entrance examination at the Academy of Art in Vienna; good and bad from the point of view of a picture-postcard painter. And it became illegal for people to utter other views about art and paintings than those of Adolf Hitler, the Supreme Führer.

Once you begin to admit that it is the duty of the government to control your consumption of alcohol, what can you reply to those who say the control of books and ideas is much more important?

Freedom to Make Mistakes

Freedom really means *the freedom to make mistakes.* This we have to realize. We may be highly critical with regard to the way in which our fellow citizens are spending their money and living their lives. We may believe that what they are doing is absolutely foolish and bad, but in a free society, there are many ways for people to air their opinions on how their fellow citizens should change their ways of life. They can write books; they can write articles; they can make speeches; they can even preach at street corners if they want—and they do this, in many countries. But they must *not* try to police other people in order to prevent them from doing certain things simply because they themselves do not want these other people to have the freedom to do it.

This is the difference between slavery and freedom. The slave must do what his superior orders him to do, but the free citizen—and this is what freedom means—is in a position to choose his own way of life. Certainly this capitalistic system can be abused, and is abused, by some people. It is certainly possible to do things which ought not to be done. But if these things are approved by a majority of the people, a disapproving person always has a way to attempt to change the minds of his fellow citizens. He can try to persuade them, to convince them, but he may not try to force them by the use of power, of governmental police power.

Status and Caste

In the market economy, everyone serves his fellow citizens by serving himself. This is what the liberal authors of the eighteenth century had in mind when they spoke of the harmony of the rightly understood interests of all groups and of all individuals of the population. And it was this doctrine of the harmony of interests which the socialists opposed. They spoke of an "irreconcilable conflict of interests" between various groups.

What does this mean? When Karl Marx—in the first chapter of the *Communist Manifesto,* that small pamphlet which inaugurated his socialist movement—claimed that there was an irreconcilable conflict between classes, he could not illustrate his thesis by any examples other than those drawn from the conditions of precapitalistic society. In precapitalistic ages, society was divided into hereditary status groups, which in India are called "castes." In a status society a man was not, for example, born a Frenchman; he was born as a member of the French aristocracy or of the French bourgeoisie or of the French peasantry. In the greater part of the Middle Ages, he was simply a serf. And serfdom, in France, did not disappear completely until after the American Revolution. In other parts of Europe it disappeared even later.

But the worst form in which serfdom existed—and continued to exist even after the abolition of slavery—was in the British colonies abroad. The individual inherited his status from his parents, and he retained it throughout his life. He transferred it to his children. Every group had privileges and disadvantages. The highest groups had only privileges, the lowest groups only disadvantages. And there was no way a man could rid himself of the legal disadvantages placed upon him by his status other than by fighting a political struggle against the other classes. Under such conditions, you could say that there was an "irreconcilable conflict of interests between the slave owners and the slaves," because what the slaves wanted was to be rid of their slavery, of their quality of being slaves. This meant a loss, however, for the owners. Therefore, there is no question that there had to be this irreconcilable conflict of interests between the members of the various classes.

One must not forget that in those ages—in which the status societies were predominant in Europe, as well as in the colonies which the Europeans later founded in America—people did not consider themselves to be connected in any special way with the other classes of their own nation; they felt much more at one with the members of their own class in other countries. A French aristocrat did not look upon lower class Frenchmen as his fellow citizens; they were the "rabble," which he did not like. He regarded only the aristocrats of other countries—those of Italy, England, and Germany, for instance—as his equals.

The most visible effect of this state of affairs was the fact that the aristocrats all over Europe used the same language. And this language was French, a language which was not understood, outside France, by other groups of the population. The middle classes—the bourgeoisie—had their own language, while the lower classes—the peasantry—used local dialects which very often were not understood by other groups of the population. The same was true with regard to the way people dressed. When you travelled in 1750 from one country to another, you found that the upper classes, the aristocrats, were usually dressed in the same way all over Europe, and you found that the lower classes dressed differently. When you met someone in the street, you could see immediately—from the way he dressed—to which class, to which status he belonged.

It is difficult to imagine how different these conditions were from present-day conditions. When I come from the United States to Argentina and I see a man on the street, I cannot know what his status is. I only assume that he is a citizen of Argentina and that he is not a member of some legally restricted group. This is one thing that capitalism has brought about. Of course, there are also differences within capitalism. There are differences in wealth, differences which Marxians mistakenly consider to be equivalent to the old differences that existed between men in the status society.

Aristocratic Wealth

The differences within a capitalist society are not the same as those in a socialist society. In the Middle Ages—and in many countries even much later—a family could be an aristocratic family and possess great wealth; it could be a family of dukes for hundreds and hundreds of years, whatever its qualities, its talents, its character or morals. But, under modern capitalistic conditions, there is what has been technically described by sociologists as "social mobility." The operating principle of this social mobility, according to the Italian sociologist and economist Vilfredo Pareto, is *la circulation des élites* (the circulation of the elites). This means that there are always people who are at the top of the social ladder, who are wealthy, who are politically important, but these people—these elites—are continually changing.

This is perfectly true in a capitalist society. It was *not* true for a precapitalistic status society. The families who were considered the great aristocratic families of Europe are still the same families today or, let us say, they are the descendants of families that were foremost in Europe, 800 or 1000 or more years ago. The Capetians of Bourbon—who for a very long time ruled here in Argentina—were a royal house as early as the tenth century. These kings ruled the territory which is known now as the Ile-de-France, extending their reign from generation to generation. But in a capitalist society, there is continuous mobility—poor people becoming rich and the descendants of those rich people losing their wealth and becoming poor.

Wealth Under Capitalism

Today I saw in a bookshop in one of the central streets of Buenos Aires the biography of a businessman who was so eminent, so important, so characteristic of big business in the nineteenth century in Europe that, even in this country, far away from Europe, the bookshop carried copies of his biography. I happen to know the grandson of this man. He has the same name his grandfather had, and he still has a right to wear the title of nobility which his grandfather—who started as a blacksmith—had received eighty years ago. Today, this grandson is a poor photographer in New York City.

Other people, who were poor at the time this photographer's grandfather became one of Europe's biggest industrialists, are today captains of industry. Everyone is free to change his status. This is the difference between the status system and the capitalist system of economic freedom, in which everyone has only himself to blame if he does not reach the position he wants to reach.

The most famous industrialist of the twentieth century up to now is Henry Ford. He started with a few hundred dollars which he had borrowed from his friends, and within a very short time he developed one of the most important big business firms of the world. And one can discover hundreds of such cases every day.

Every day, the *New York Times* prints long notices of people who have died. If you read these biographies, you may come across the name of an eminent businessman, who started out as a seller of newspapers at street corners in New York. Or he started as an office boy, and at his death he was the president of the same banking firm where he started on the lowest rung of the ladder. Of course, not all people can attain these positions. Not all people *want* to attain them. There are people who are more interested in other problems and, for these people, other ways are open today which were not open in the days of feudal society, in the ages of the status society.

The socialist system, however, *forbids* this fundamental freedom to choose one's own career. Under socialist conditions, there is only one economic authority, and it has the right to determine all matters concerning production.

Central Planning

One of the characteristic features of our day is that people use many names for the same thing. One synonym for socialism and communism is "planning." If people speak of "planning" they mean, of course, *central* planning, which means *one plan made by the government*—one plan that prevents planning by anyone except the government.

A British lady, who also is a member of the Upper House, wrote a book entitled *Plan or No Plan,* a book which was quite popular around the world. What does the title of her book mean? When she says "plan," she means only the type of plan envisioned by Lenin and Stalin and their successors, the type which governs all the activities of all the people of a nation. Thus, this lady means a central plan which excludes all the personal plans that individuals may have. Her title *Plan or No Plan is* therefore an illusion, a deception; the alternative is not a central plan or no plan, it is *the total plan* of a central governmental authority *or freedom* for individuals to make their own plans, to do their own planning. The individual plans his life, every day, changing his daily plans whenever he will.

The free man plans daily for his needs; he says, for example:

"Yesterday I planned to work all my life in Córdoba." Now he learns about better conditions in Buenos Aires and changes his plans, saying: "Instead of working in Córdoba, I want to go to Buenos Aires." And that is what freedom means. It may be that he is mistaken; it may be that his going to Buenos Aires will turn out to have been a mistake. Conditions may have been better for him in Córdoba, but he himself made his plans.

Under government planning, he is like a soldier in an army. The soldier in the army does not have the right to choose his garrison, to choose the place where he will serve. He has to obey orders. And the socialist system—as Karl Marx, Lenin, and all socialist leaders knew and admitted—is the transfer of army rule to the whole production system. Marx spoke of "industrial armies," and Lenin called for "the organization of everything—the postoffice, the factory, and other industries, according to the model of the army."

Therefore, in the socialist system everything depends on the wisdom, the talents, and the gifts of those people who form the supreme authority. That which the supreme dictator—or his committee—does *not* know, is not taken into account. But the knowledge which mankind has accumulated in its long history is not acquired by everyone; we have accumulated such an enormous amount of scientific and technological knowledge over the centuries that it is humanly impossible for one individual to know all these things, even though he be a most gifted man.

And people are different; they are unequal. They always will be. There are some people who are more gifted in one subject and less in another one. And there are people who have the gift to find new paths, to change the trend of knowledge. In capitalist societies, technological progress and economic progress are gained through such people. If a man has an idea, he will try to find a few people who are clever enough to realize the value of his idea. Some capitalists, who dare to look into the future, who realize the possible consequences of such an idea, will start to put it to work. Other people, at first, may say: "They are fools"; but they will stop saying so when they discover that this enterprise, which they called foolish, is flourishing, and that people are happy to buy its products.

The Buyer as Boss vs. Control by a "Planner"

Under the Marxian system, on the other hand, the supreme government body must first be convinced of the value of such an idea before it can be pursued and developed. This can be a very difficult thing to do, for only the group of people at the head—or the supreme dictator himself—has the power to make decisions. And if these people—because of laziness or old age, or because they are not very bright and learned—are unable to grasp the importance of the new idea, then the new project will not be undertaken. . . .

In the United States you hear of something new, of some improvement, almost every week. These are improvements that business has generated, because thousands and thousands of business people are trying day and night to find some new product which satisfies the consumer better or is less expensive to produce, or better *and* less expensive than the existing products. They do not do this out of altruism; they do it because they want to make money. And the effect is that you have an improvement in the standard of living in the United States which is almost miraculous, when compared with the conditions that existed fifty or a hundred years ago. But in Soviet Russia, where you do not have such a system, you do not have a comparable improvement. So those people who tell us that we ought to adopt the Soviet system are badly mistaken.

There is something else that should be mentioned. The American consumer, the individual, is both a buyer and a boss. When you leave a store in America, you may find a sign saying: "Thank you for your patronage. Please come again." But when you go into a shop in a totalitarian country—be it in present-day [1959] Russia, or in Germany as it was under the regime of Hitler—the shopkeeper tells you: "You have to be thankful to the great leader for giving you this."

In socialist countries, it is not the seller who has to be grateful, it is the buyer. The citizen is *not* the boss; the boss is the Central Committee, the Central Office. Those socialist committees and leaders and dictators are supreme, and the people simply have to obey them.

The Ugly Market

by Israel M. Kirzner

One of the most intriguing paradoxes surrounding modern capitalism is the hate, the fear, and the contempt with which it is commonly regarded. Every ill in contemporary society is invariably blamed on business, on the pursuit of private profit, on the institution of private ownership. Those who have pierced the shrouds of hate and ignorance with which the critics of the market have enveloped it, inevitably come to ask themselves why so valuable a social institution is held in such universal contempt and dislike. The question is one which has a scientific fascination of its own. But the question has significance extending far beyond mere scientific curiosity. As Mises pointed out, "A social system, however beneficial, cannot work if it is not supported by public opinion."[1]

Those who are convinced that the market system is uniquely capable of mobilizing and developing the resources available to a society in a manner able most faithfully to reflect the wishes of its members, while it protects and nourishes their political and economic liberties, have for a long time been aware of the unfortunate validity of this statement. The ability of the market to serve society has been and is continually being undermined by the attacks levelled by its ideological opponents and by the powerlessness of the public to withstand these attacks. Public opinion has come to be moulded in a direction overwhelmingly antithetical to a market orientation. The "anti-capitalist mentality" has come to pervade the thinking of the masses who are the market's chief beneficiaries, of the intellectuals and social scientists who might have been expected to be its principal interpreters and exponents, as well as of the entrepreneurs and business leaders who constitute its pivotal instruments. It is surely a tribute to the extraordinary vitality and power of the market system that in the face of such deep mistrust,

---

Dr. Kirzner, author of such important works as *Competition and Entrepreneurship* and *The Economic Point of View*, is professor of economics at New York University and a frequent lecturer at FEE seminars. This article originally appeared in the December 1974 issue of *The Freeman*.

and in the teeth of massive and well-nigh crippling state interventions (deriving largely from this anti-capitalist mentality), the system still continues to support an enormously complex division of labor and to generate an unprecedentedly high flow of goods and services. How long this can be continued in the face of widespread lack of confidence in the efficiency and morality of the system, must seriously trouble those concerned for the very survival of the system.

An understanding of the nature and sources of this anti-capitalist mentality is, therefore, crucially important. If this mentality is to be dispelled, its principal features must be clearly pointed out, and its sources identified. A number of scholars have addressed themselves to this task. A series of papers by various writers was published under the editorship of Hayek two decades ago,[2] drawing attention to the anti-capitalist bias of historians, and relating this to the hostility towards the early emergence of capitalism in the eighteenth and nineteenth centuries evinced at the time by the aristocracy and the intellectuals. Almost four decades ago Hutt[3] brilliantly analyzed the causes, not so much of the existence of the anti-capitalist mentality itself, as of the surprising inability of the economists to influence public opinion towards an appreciation of the beneficent operation of the competitive market process. More recently both Mises[4] and Stigler[5] have sought to explain the emergence of the strong antipathies shown towards the market system by so many, including the intellectuals who might have been expected to be its most enthusiastic supporters. Historians of economic thought have, and no doubt will, chart the vagaries in the attitudes of economists themselves towards the social usefulness of a decentralized system of decision-making based on private property.

The following discussion of the anti-capitalist mentality will attempt to identify three distinct levels at which this mentality demands analysis: *First*, we will notice the objections explicitly raised by the critics of capitalism. It is through these charges, criticisms, and denunciations that the anti-capitalist mentality finds overt expression. *Second*, we will identify the analytical premises which inform (or misinform) the stated criticisms expressive of the anti-capitalist mentality. Any attempt to respond to the criticism raised at the first level must sooner or later search out the weaknesses of the analytical bases—at the second level—for these criticisms. *Third*, we will take note of the deeper attitudes which have inspired the various forms of anti-capitalist mentality. Whatever the stated, specific denunciations of capitalism, whatever the errors in economic analysis which are implicit in these denunciations, a thorough understanding of the anti-capitalist mentality cannot avoid ultimately coming to grips with the deep-seated prejudices and engrained habits of thought which are, both consciously and unconsciously, responsible for the antipathy shown to the market system. We will now take up in turn the three levels which we have identified.

The Stated Criticisms

The list of denunciations of the market system is both well-known and long. They range from those which condemn the system on moral grounds to those which attack it on more narrowly economic grounds. We will make no attempt to do more than merely recite this list. It is not our main purpose here to grapple with these criticisms. Rather we list them to indicate the range of expression of the anti-capitalist mentality, and more importantly, to distinguish these stated criticisms sharply from their theoretical underpinnings, and from the unstated attitudes to which they are, in large measure, to be ascribed.

The market system is indicted as feeding and responsible for the *materialistic aspects* of modern society. It is blamed as promoting and permitting the expression of *selfishness* and *greed*. It is charged with *encouraging fraudulent behavior*. It is denounced as *debasing the tastes of the public* through advertising, fraudulent or otherwise, leading them to demand products and services which are in fact *harmful and degenerating*. The system is held accountable for the *destruction of the environment*. It is denounced for *destroying the self-esteem* of its workers, for generating profound *alienation, despondency and despair* within society, as well as for widespread *insecurity and anxieties*. The *inequality in incomes* which characterizes capitalist countries is denounced as evil in itself and socially deleterious in its consequences. This inequality is condemned as exemplifying the fundamental *injustice* of the market system; it is perceived as expressive of economic *oppression* and *exploitation*. The market system is made to shoulder responsibility for *racism,* for *sexism,* for *imperialism.* The market is given failing grades in its strictly economic functions. It is seen as producing shoddy, dangerous products for the *profit of the businessman rather than for the use of the consumer.* It is seen as generating cataclysmic spasms of *overproduction, unemployment and monetary crisis.* It is seen as *subverting the operation of political democracy.* It is blamed for the corruption of government and for the *concentrations of dangerous centers of economic power in big business.*

No doubt this list is an incomplete one. But it does present the range of anti-capitalist clichés with which we are all familiar. Sooner or later the anti-capitalist mentality expresses itself in one or several of these charges, denunciations and criticisms.

Before reviewing the *theoretical bases* for these criticisms, it is important that one observation be made. This is that while in most cases these denunciations can be sustained only in the context of particular theoretical views (so that the revelation of fallacies in these views renders these objections harmless) the objections themselves are usually raised without benefit of *any explicit* theoretical framework. An undesirable aspect of capitalist reality is observed, whether it is the prevalence of fraud or unemployment, or racism, or greed. This aspect is then uncritically attributed to capitalism itself. The circumstance that, in the nature of things, undesirable features of capitalist reality—or, for that matter, of any reality—abound, must in some measure account for the continual reappearance of old denunciations of capitalism in new guises despite their earlier refutations.

Anti-Capitalist Theory—The Stigler-Zweig Thesis

We now turn, then, to examine the theoretical bases which nourish the overt denunciations of the market system listed in the preceding section. In this we confine ourselves to those (often merely implicit) views of anti-capitalists which seem most clearly vulnerable to critical scrutiny. It is not, to repeat, our purpose here substantively to deal with the objections listed in the preceding section. Nor, in fact, do we necessarily maintain that each and every one of these objections is entirely without force. But in examining the analytical "vision" expressed by the anti-capitalist mentality, we find it expedient to draw attention only to those aspects of it which, we believe, dispassionate consideration reveals to be flawed.

In fact our purpose in setting forth the theoretical underpinnings of anti-capitalism is to illustrate what may be termed the Stigler-Zweig thesis.

This thesis is that the traditional training of the professional economist predisposes him towards a free enterprise view on economic affairs. This thesis has support from more than one quarter within the ideological spectrum. In a well-known paper a dozen years ago, Stigler advanced this thesis: "the professional study of economics makes one politically conservative" (with a "conservative" defined as one "who wishes most economic activity to be conducted by private enterprise, and who believes that abuses of private power will usually be checked, and incitements to efficiency and progress usually provided, by the forces of competition")[6]. More recently Michael Zweig has expressed, on behalf of the New Left, the similar view long held by socialist critics of orthodox economics: that marginalist analysis (with which orthodox economics is held to be completely identified) is not only "irrelevant," but that it can be "pernicious," so that "marginalism is fundamentally counterrevolutionary."[7] In an essay introducing a volume of readings which includes many contributions from both the New and Old Left, Lekachman, too, has registered his opinion that marginalism is "a highly conservative notion."[8]

Our survey of the theoretical groundwork of the anti-capitalist mentality will confirm this thesis. We will discover, that is, that this theoretical vision is inconsistent (to say the least) with that which underlies economic analysis. So that *this* level of discussion of the anti-capitalist mentality must perceive it, as Mises has insisted again and again, as the *denial of economic science.*

It is to be observed that the Stigler-Zweig thesis, or a variant of it, is relevant not only to the theoretical bases for these anti-capitalist objections which are strictly economic in character, but also to those which underlie the denunciations concerned with the morality of the market system. The habits of thought engendered by economic analysis enable one to avoid ethical judgments which are mutually inconsistent or which otherwise rest on logically invalid foundations.

If the preceding section consisted of a list of well-worn denunciations of capitalism, the following pages will turn out to offer a catalogue of those fallacies which teachers of introductory economic theory find themselves again and again forced to unmask.

(a) *One man's gain must be another's loss*: Innocence of economics is often most clearly manifested by the refusal to recognize that free exchange must have been viewed as (at least prospectively) beneficial by both sides to the deal. The error of insisting that gain in the market must be at someone else's expense is responsible for a wide range of denunciations of the market. These include charges of exploitation of sellers by buyers (as in the case of labor), and of exploitation of buyers by sellers (as in the case of landlord relations). This error is responsible for the perennial willingness of critics of capitalism to prohibit exchanges in which they perceive one of the parties to be receiving inordinate benefit. The error is, further, one of the foundations for the condemnation of profits in general, and thus of the entire market system insofar as it is the social manifestation of the profit motive.

(b) *Blaming the waiter for obesity*: Failure to perceive the degree to which the notion of consumer sovereignty manifests itself in the market is responsible for what Stigler has called blaming the waiter for obesity. In the most naive forms of this fallacy, the market system is condemned for the efficiency and abundance with which it ministers to consumer tastes which the critic does not share. To a large degree the condemnation of capitalism for "materialism" reflects this aberration. (One recalls that not only the market has been condemned for its materialism, but economists have been denounced for their interest in such a debased topic as the material side of human existence.) To some degree the condemnation of business for producing shoddy or dangerous products reflects a failure to understand that consumers are simply unwilling to sacrifice as much as would be necessary to enjoy a higher level of quality and safety. There can be no doubt that current denunciations of capitalism for its effect upon the environment must, to some extent, be seen as reflecting a value placed upon the quality of the environment which is higher than that placed by consumers in general.

To a certain extent, the charges of racism and sexism levelled against capitalism are expressive of the same blindness towards the direction in which causes and effects are related in the market process. At somewhat less naive levels of discussion, the "blaming the waiter for obesity" fallacy resurfaces as an attack on advertising and selling effort in general. If it is not the waiter himself who is to be the culprit, it is the neon sign outside the restaurant, or the tempting aroma of good food escaping therefrom, which are perceived as the villains. It is perhaps because elementary economics in fact generally fails to make clear the role of selling effort in the entrepreneurial process of seeking to serve the market, that this particular form of the obesity fallacy is advanced so triumphantly by economists who ought to know better.

(c) *Petulance at costs (or the denial of scarcity)*: To a surprising extent the criticisms of anti-capitalists turn out to reflect merely an impatience at the costs inevitably associated with the achievement of desired goals. Again and again undesirable features of the economic landscape are cited as evidence of the failure of the market. (Incidentally, the same fallacy is, to be sure, often committed in the course of procapitalist criticisms of socialist economies.) Here it is not so much that the critic ignores or disagrees with the values of consumers, as that he simply refuses to recognize that efficiency in achieving more highly valued goals may necessitate the deliberate renunciation of otherwise important goals which happen to be less urgently valued. Long working hours, poor working conditions, loss of pristine environmental beauty may, elementary economics teaches us, be evidence not of the failure of the economic system (whether capitalist or socialist) to achieve its goals, but of the very efficiency with which it channels resources away from less crucial goals towards those more highly valued. Some aspects of what the critics deplore as worker alienation, or of the anxiety and insecurity felt by market participants, would surely be appraised rather differently were they recognized as the inevitable costs of division of labor or of a social system in which freedom of entry for competitors is the prime motive force. At a somewhat more subtle level, the often deplored garishness and pervasiveness of modern advertising take on a different aspect when perceived as a social cost made necessary by the sheer multitude of products from which the consumer in successful capitalism must choose. The very affluence of capitalism, it turns out, reveals a new guise in which scarcity manifests itself—the scarcity of information on what to consume out of the available riches. Anti-capitalist critics—it turns out—are ill-equipped to perceive these insights of elementary economics.

(d) *The fear of anarchy*: As Hayek has repeatedly pointed out, one of the clichés of our age sees a blemish in anything that "is not consciously directed as a whole," that this is a "proof of its irrationality and of the need completely to replace it by a deliberately designed mechanism."[9] In particular, this fallacy is related to "the inability, caused by the lack of a compositive theory of social phenomena, to grasp how the independent action of many men can produce coherent wholes, persistent structures of relationships which serve important human purposes without having been designed for that end."[10]

There can be no doubt that this "lack of compositive theory of social phenomena" is the view underlying an enormous volume of anti-capitalist criticism. The anti-capitalist mentality, it is clear, is to a great extent, coextensive with ignorance of, or a refusal to acknowledge, the insights into the market *system* which economics theory reveals. Once it is taken for granted that a society unplanned from the top must generate incessant chaos, it becomes easy enough to seize on targets that may be held to exemplify that chaos. Even where critics of capitalism recognize the determinateness of market forces, they see them as nonetheless chaotic in the sense that these forces are believed to lead in socially undesirable directions.

(e) *Fear of the consequences of greed*: Closely related to the preceding analytical prejudice is that which tends to attribute undesirable consequences to the market simply because the market permits greedy or selfish individuals to act out their impulses. Because freedom to trade means freedom to act greedily or selfishly, it is believed the consequences of laissez-faire must inevitably tend to be nasty, brutish and jungle-like. What is being implicitly denied in this respect is the ability of the market process to harness the greed of its participants so as to serve the wishes of the other participants. Refusal to perceive the constraints upon individual actions imposed by the market permits anti-capitalists to interpret those aspects of the economics landscape which they deplore as the only-to-be-expected, sinister consequences of a social system based on selfishness and greed.

(f) *Blaming the market for the results of intervention:* As is well known, the market system is frequently criticized for features of contemporary economic society which are, in fact, to be attributed to state *interference* with the market. Of course, to the extent that it is *contemporary* capitalism which is being attacked, there can be no objection to this. However, such criticisms of capitalism, it all too frequently turns out, are in fact deployed to attack not the statist interference with the market process, but the market system itself. We have here a simple analytical failure to recognize, within the complex tangle of modern capitalism, the consequences of its market elements, from those of non-market admixtures. This analytical failure manifests itself in many of those objections to capitalism which relate to absence of competition generated by government-imposed barriers to entry (or from limitations on international trade), or to maladjustments arising from government price controls of various kinds or to cyclical maladjustments (including large-scale unemployment) generated by massive government monetary expansion. In all such criticisms, what is at issue is the theory maintained (perhaps implicitly) by the critics that the undesirable features being exposed are to be attributed, not to departures from the market, but to the untrammeled workings of the market process itself.

(g) *The "Nirvana Fallacy"*: As the final entry in our (doubtless incomplete) list of analytical fallacies, we present what Professor Demsetz has labeled the "Nirvana Approach."[11] (In fact we will present it in a somewhat broader context than that identified by Demsetz). Demsetz explains that "those who adopt the Nirvana viewpoint seek to discover discrepancies between the ideal and the real and if discrepancies are found, they deduce that the real is inefficient."[12] There can be no doubt that many critics of capitalism are judging its efficiency and/or morality by comparison with some ideal norm that can have little relevance for real problems. In so doing they overlook the fact that improving an imperfect world must take place against the background of that imperfect world; that it is usually simply impossible to remake whole systems in their entirety; that even where this is possible, the costs of doing so may make imperfection relatively attractive and efficient.

The nirvana attitude of many anti-capitalists manifests itself in various ways. Thus the market is frequently blamed for the distribution of incomes to which it gives rise without regard to the circumstance that the market presupposes some initial distribution of resource ownership (especially in regard to the resources embodied in human beings themselves). Or, where marginal analysis is indicted for accepting without challenge the institutional structure (including the existing property rights system) within which marginal adjustments are contemplated to be made, there is no awareness on the part of the critics, of the *costs* (transaction and policing) of remaking the social system from the very foundations. Or, again, as Demsetz has shown, critics who have pointed to externalities or other circumstances spelling inefficiency, have frequently ignored, in their calculations, the cost of resources that would be required to correct these inefficiencies.

The Sources of the Anti-Capitalist Mentality

Our survey of anti-capitalist criticisms of the market, and our identification of the analytical confusions which have frequently supported these criticisms make it of special interest to review now the underlying psychological attitudes and prejudices which might fuel this mentality. The very recognition of the confusions which abound in the theoretical underpinnings for so much anti-capitalist criticism, makes it clear that such criticism must be nourished by deeply held values and prejudices. The literature cited earlier in this paper, together with several additional sources, yield the following inventory of attitudes from which anti-capitalism might easily be expected to spring.

(a) Mises has dwelt at length on the *resentments* which can arise from *frustrated ambitions*, of the *envy* on the part of the intellectuals and the white-collar workers of the good fortunes enjoyed by successful entrepreneurs.

(b) Similar in important respects must be judged the widespread views that economic inequalities are somehow immoral and seriously undesirable per se. Here the often vicarious envy of the wealthy and sympathy for the poor must be judged as predisposing observers of capitalist inequalities towards "sinister" interpretations of the sources of these inequalities.

(c) Deep-seated contempt for greed and for self-centered activities is clearly responsible for a readiness to believe the worst about capitalism.[13]

(d) An almost similarly deep-seated contempt for the low tastes of the masses and thus for the businessmen who cater to these low tastes is responsible for treating the *market* as vulgar and crass. It becomes, in fact, all the easier to blame the vulgarity of mass tastes upon the businessmen who minister to them.

(e) Closely related to high-brow disdain of mass tastes, must be listed man's love for the natural over the artificial, his preference for more spaciousness and simplicity over urban congestion and complexity. Since the spectacular success of industrial capitalism was accompanied by the loss of the simple, natural life for which so many of us yearn, capitalism itself has come to be the villain.[14]

(f) And again, the yearning for simplicity abuts on the deep-rooted unwillingness of men to be forced to be efficient. Modern capitalism is despised and feared because it successfully mobilizes available resources to serve socially needed purposes.

(g) Widespread *fear of economic power* must be considered one of the attitudes responsible for anti-capitalism. While what Professor Petro has recently called the "economic power syndrome"[15] is often accompanied by an explicit theoretical position which denies the role of consumer sovereignty, it seems clear that in many instances the syndrome in fact *precedes* the theoretical position needed to support it. Thus the very success of capitalism in organizing production in efficient, large-scale productive units is responsible, in fact, for the suspicions which have led to its being so bitterly attacked.

(h) Professor Hutt has pointed out that opponents of economics are often the victims of what he calls "custom-thought"[16]—intellectual inertness. To be sure custom-thought may work in more than one direction. But the long list in the preceding section of this paper of economic fallacies subscribed to by anti-capitalists suggests that intellectual inertness might indeed play a not insignificant role in the anti-capitalist mentality.

(i) Finally we notice, as an explanation for the persistence of so many elementary fallacies, the role of the "corruption of opinion by interest." Professor Hutt[17] has provided a full review of the role of "power thought" in this regard. Here again, of course, opinion can be corrupted by interest in more than one direction. But when one thinks of the businessmen who stand to gain from governmental protection against domestic or foreign competition and of the many who, rightly or wrongly, believe that a different order of things would redound to their benefit, it cannot be denied that this must be counted an important source of anti-capitalism.

Wrestling with the Anti-Capitalist Mentality

Traditionally apologists for capitalism have addressed themselves to the specific stated objections and accusations advanced by the detractors of the market. In attempting to do this they have, of course, found it necessary to search out the logical fallacies which support these objections. At the same time awareness of the more deeply rooted prejudices which seem to be responsible for the continued vitality of the anticapitalist mentality, raise doubts as to the efficacy of this strategy for the ideological defense of the market. Recognition of the three-level character of the anti-capitalist mentality emphasized in this paper can be of help in identifying what must be faced. At the level of stated objections, there is an enormous variety of possible manifestations of the mentality. Refutation of one particular objection in one form does not prevent its reappearance in some other form. Clearly, for this reason, theory has a crucial role to play in refuting the analytical fallacies responsible for entire groups of possible objections and denunciations of the market. On the other hand, the very generality of theoretical discussion makes it possible for critics of capitalism to fail to see how the theories relate to *particular* features of the market which seem to invite criticism. The proper *application* of theory is, of course, in many ways more difficult than theorizing itself.

Moreover, economic theory is for various reasons not well-adapted for the task of combating anti-capitalism. Theorists are scientists whose attempts at maintaining *value-freedom* in their work seem to render them unprepared to serve as apologists for a particular system of social organization. Again, the *sophistication* of modern theory is hardly conducive to the correction of popular misconceptions. (We recall that Edwin Cannan, for this reason, appealed for *simple* economics). There are grounds for believing that the character of much contemporary theory, especially in its emphasis on equilibrium conditions, is not well-suited for the explication of the social function of the market.[18] At the ideological level defense against the anticapitalist mentality seems to require continual new applications of fundamental theory to new situations.

But on the other hand, our awareness of the role of theoretical fallacy and of the impact of the multitude of specific denunciations of the market, must make us cautious in imagining that the anti-capitalist mentality can be dispelled by any device that fails to come to grips with each of these levels of its manifestation. No matter how successfully one or more of the underlying anti-capitalist prejudices may be neutralized, the possibility of logical error yet remains and the availability of apparently undesirable features of capitalism ready to be used in its denunciation has not yet been eliminated. Moreover, the formidable list of anti-capitalist prejudices must raise doubts concerning the likelihood that they can be successfully neutralized by any simple means. To be sure, any advance is desirable if its costs are acceptable. But the degree of advance needed to make a visible dent in the anti-capitalist mentality must require the most careful examination of the costs involved in any proposal.

Many students of capitalism have pointed out that, despite its advantages, there may well be grounds for predicting its replacement by other systems. One thinks of Schumpeter's thesis in this regard. One possible reason for arguing that capitalism is unstable is that it is a social system which generates a negative public opinion so powerful as to spell its ultimate death. This paper has attempted to identify the sources of this tendency. Only by recognizing the nature and the power of these forces can we hope, through patient teaching and discussion, to dispel the hate and the ignorance which surround the free market.

---

1. Ludwig von Mises, *Human Action* (New Haven, Conn.: Yale University Press, 1949), p. 861.
2. F. A. Hayek (Ed.), *Capitalism and the Historians* (Chicago: University of Chicago Press, 1954).
3. W. H. Hutt, *Economists and the Public, A Study of Competition and Opinion* (London: J. Cape, 1936).
4. Ludwig von Mises, *The Anti-Capitalistic Mentality* (South Holland, Ill.: Libertarian Press, 1972).
5. George J. Stigler, "The Intellectual and the Market Place," *National Review*, December 1963.
6. George J. Stigler, "The Politics of Political Economists," *Quarterly Journal of Economics*, November 1959; reprinted in *Essays in the History of Economics* (Chicago: University of Chicago Press, 1965), pp. 52–53.
7. M. Zweig, "A New Left Critique of Economics," in D. Mermelstein (Ed.), *Economics: Mainstream Readings and Radical Critiques* (New York: 1970), p. 25.
8. R. Lekachman, "Special Introduction" in Mermelstein, p. xi.

9. F. A. Hayek, *The Counter-Revolution of Science* (Glencoe, Ill.: Free Press, 1955), p. 87.

10. *Ibid.*, p. 80 (italics supplied). See also F. A. Hayek, *Individualism and Economic Order* (London: Routledge and Kegan Paul, 1949), pp. 7 ff.

11. H. Demsetz, "Information and Efficiency: Another Viewpoint," *Journal of Law and Economics*, April 1969.

12. *Ibid.*, p. 1.

13. One thinks here in particular of Ruskin.

14. See the above cited *Capitalism and the Historians.*

15. See Sylvester Petro, "The Economic-Power Syndrome," in the Mises *Festschrift*, *Toward Liberty* (Menlo Park, Cal.: Institute for Humane Studies, 1971), Vol. II, p. 274.

16. Hutt, p. 50.

17. *Ibid.*, Chapters III and IV.

18. One thinks here in particular of Professor Buchanan's plea that economics be understood as a sophisticated catallactics, the theory of exchanges and of markets. See his "What Should Economists Do?", *Southern Economic Journal*, January 1964.

Is There a Moral Basis for Capitalism?

by Charles Dykes

The contemporary indictment of capitalism usually takes two basic forms. First, there is the economic indictment. Those who make the attack from this perspective argue that capitalism is not viable because it is afflicted with insurmountable contradictions which result in a permanent state of crisis, or problems which can be resolved only temporarily by palliatives. Second, there is the *moral* indictment. Capitalism, according to this view, is the exploitation of man by man, the profit motive and the rule of money supreme, with an inevitable cruel injustice everywhere manifest.

The claim that capitalism provides the best economic structure for man's moral development, long a virtual article of faith in American life, is met with derision these days by politicians, journalists, university professors, and theologians. Clergymen daily rage with indignation against the "evils" and "injustice" of the competitive market. Capitalism is, so we are told, "intrinsically immoral." "Soul dead, stomach well alive," was Thomas Carlyle's estimate of the market system, and all the cultured despisers of commercial civilization are in hearty agreement.

The market order, we are informed, promotes a materialistic view of life. "Things," Emerson once said bitterly, "are in the saddle and ride mankind." The capitalistic form of economic organization is said to be dehumanizing. Owen Chadwick has brilliantly summarized the thought of Karl Marx for us on this point: "The structure of society derives from the work which men do. In bourgeois society the worker provides goods, to serve not the needs of men but the needs of the market. Then, instead of men controlling goods, goods control men; so that, the more workers produce, the wider the gap between rich and poor. This ill-arrangement may be called the 'alienation' of man's work. A man's work is 'natural,' part of the structure of living. Therefore

---

Mr. Dykes has contributed a number of thoughtful articles to *The Freeman*. He is an active businessman based in Mississippi. This article originally appeared in the August 1983 issue of *The Freeman*.

the alienation of his work creates an alienation of man from nature, from his fellow-worker, even from himself. Economic nonsense pushed all relations awry. Men and women become things and treat each other like things."[1]

Hostility Against Capitalism

The animus of many theologians against capitalism is especially bitter. Michael Novak gives a not uncommon example: "Jurgen Moltmann portrays capitalism as though it were outside the law, destructive of true community, reducing all relations to impersonal monetary relations, inspiring wolf-like animosity between man and man and irrational in its pursuit of growth for the sake of growth and work for the sake of work."[2]

Writing in *The Christian Century* in 1976, Bruce Douglass admits that most of the political and economic comment coming from theologians has a socialist flavor. He then goes on to insist that defenders of capitalism are engaged in what amounts to a justification of injustice, selfishness, and other forms of sin. The case for socialism, we are given to understand, is primarily concerned with justice, and is thus exactly the opposite.

What of these charges? Does capitalism "make the world free for sinners," at the same time relentlessly alienating man from his fellows and himself, even as it dehumanizes him? Does it unleash, and then callously celebrate as virtue, a rampant and rapacious selfishness? Is it oblivious to, indeed destructive of, the demands of justice in human relations? Is it, in sum, without moral justification, and thus guilty as charged of being "intrinsically immoral"?

It is our conviction that these charges are entirely fallacious. Not only that: We are soundly convinced the market economy is securely anchored to the Judeo-Christian revelation. Neither the caricatures of its enemies, nor the perversions of its friends, can alter this fact.

A System of Relationships

The critics are right when they demand that our economic system rest on a firm moral basis. If it can be shown that it does not, then we should abandon it immediately and seek to establish a more just order. At the outset, however, important distinctions and clarifications must be made. Arthur Shenfield calls attention to one of the most vital, viz., "the economic system called capitalism is a system of relationships. It is a composition of markets, and markets are by definition systems of relationships, not purposive bodies. It follows that we can apply the tests of morality to capitalism only by considering the behavior of individuals who operate within it, not as a system capable in itself of being moral or immoral."

It is Shenfield's contention that since capitalism is "a system of relationships it cannot be moral or immoral in the sense that a purposive group can be. . . ." He denies, however, that such a system is morally neutral. "If its essential characteristics on balance positively nurture or reinforce moral or immoral individual behavior, it is a moral or immoral system in its effects."[3]

Furthermore, we must repudiate the erroneous tendency of many critics to attribute to capitalistic economic phenomena human behavior, social ills, or political crimes to which history bore witness before the birth of the capitalist system. And again, enemies of capitalism are prone to identify the market economy with society as a whole. For them, capitalism forms and permeates the whole of society, and in so doing destroys and corrupts human relationships other than those contracted for strictly economic purposes. But the truth is, the competitive market is only a part or aspect of any society.

"The market," as John Davenport correctly observes, "is not an end in itself, but the means to higher ends." The market is merely an element in a society which transcends and extends far beyond it. The market is but a method of recording consumer preferences and allocating resources, an information system which transmits knowledge spontaneously through the signals sent out by prices.

Allocation of Scarce Resources

All economic goods are, by definition, scarce, while the hunger of man for these goods is nearly infinite. Thus a workable economic system concerns the allocation of scarce resources—e.g., labor, materials, or capital—to human wants. Socialism assigns to a supposed omnicompetent state the task of deciding what people *need,* and then the development of a master plan as to what goods will be produced in what amounts. In the market economy, on the other hand, consumers bid on what they *want* via the price mechanism.

No matter what system a society employs for organizing its

economic life, certain common decisions must be made. For example, all economies must decide what goods will be produced, and how the fruits of this production will be distributed. All economic systems coordinate men and materials in making these decisions in some way. The market system makes these decisions and achieves this coordination through an institution of private property rights and voluntary exchange.

From the days of Adam Smith, advocates of the free market have argued that market processes have a strong tendency to equate public benefits and private profits. Following the argument of Bernard Mandeville's *Fable of the Bees*, Smith held that private vices—e.g., greed—are converted into public benefits.

A Harmony of Interests

There is, in a free market, a harmony of interests between the public and the private. Does this imply, then, that the free market, in some way, nurtures or reinforces unjust rather than just behavior? Not at all. The free market economy is the most productive form of economic organization just because it is most consistent with eternal moral principles. The economy of any society is integrally related to the moral principles and consequent values to which the society is committed and substantially adheres. Or, as Paul Johnson puts it, "The level of social morality is directly linked to the performance of the economy."[4]

Consider the testimony of Wilhelm Roepke, one of the greatest economists of the twentieth century. He wrote: "One of the most dangerous errors of our time is to believe that economic freedom and the society which is based upon it are hardly compatible with the moral standards of a strictly Christian attitude." In Roepke's view, "the very opposite of this popular belief is true: the strongest reasons to defend economic freedom and the market economy are precisely of a moral character. It is economic freedom and the market economy which the moral standards of Christianity require, not the opposite economic system. At the same time, however, we have to say with equal force that economic freedom and the market economy require these moral standards. One conditions the other."

Roepke understood that "Socialists and non-socialists are divided by fundamentally different concepts of life and life's meaning. What we judge man's position in the universe to be will in the end decide whether we believe our highest values to be realized in man or in society, and our decision for either the former or the latter will also be the watershed of our political thinking. Once more we find Cardinal Manning's famous statement to be true: "All human differences are ultimately religious ones.'" The conclusion: "We should stand for a free economic order even if it implied material sacrifice and if socialism gave the certain prospect of material increase. It is our undeserved luck that the exact opposite is true."[5]

The Family Unit

While keeping in mind that the market economy is only a part or aspect of society, we do contend that capitalism is more than just an economic system of voluntary relationships. Specifically, it is an economic system based on the right of private ownership of property and a free market for goods and services, consistent with the second table of the moral law.

The fifth commandment of the Decalogue, "Honor thy father and thy mother," implies that the family, not the state, is the basic social and economic unit of society and should be the strongest. R. J. Rushdoony has noted that "throughout history the basic welfare agency has been the family. The family, in providing for its sick and needy members, in educating children, caring for parents, and in coping with emergencies and disasters, has done and is doing more than the state has ever done or can do."[6] A society characterized by a significant degree of economic freedom is always a society dominated by strong family units who provide for their own. This contrasts with socialism, whose basic goals, if realized, would destroy the family in the interests of the larger collective.

The sixth commandment, "Thou shalt not kill," is, according to John Chamberlain, "simply the other face of Locke's and Jefferson's 'unalienable' right to life."[7] John Calvin explained it this way: "The sum of this commandment is, that we should not unjustly do violence to anyone." "Thou shalt not kill" is thus a generic expression which also forbids wounding, violent threatening, and any unjust coercion by an individual, group, or state that would restrain legitimate liberty.

Economic freedom is born and thrives only in nations or communities where reverence for all human life is widely held to be a supreme value, where the personal safety of the neighbor and his family is generally regarded as inviolably sacred, and where compassionate individuals, acting either alone or through voluntary associations, are encouraged to offer substantial assistance to the poor and needy. This differs radically from the command society of socialism, whose adherents are frequently found not only approving but actively promoting violence, terrorism, and the destruction of the middle class. In such societies (and this would include the Welfare State) "compassion" is institutionalized, and becomes a monopoly of the state.

The seventh commandment, "Thou shalt not commit adultery," teaches us, as does the ninth commandment, that contracts must be honored and double-dealing scorned. "The historic link between the biblical idea of binding covenants and the Western idea of binding contracts" writes Gary North, "is obvious enough."[8] The very idea of contracting for joint benefit presupposes a high level of moral integrity and faithfulness on the part of all the parties engaged in the transaction.

In socialism the paternal state seeks to vitiate the necessity for the sanctity of contracts by substituting its omnipotent controls and decrees. Opportunity for moral development and the growth of trust between free men is thereby suppressed. The socialist ethic in this area is readily illustrated in the attitude of contemporary socialist bloc nations toward the fulfillment of treaty obligations. The Soviet Union, for example, violated every treaty it ever made. Lacking an unchanging moral foundation, there is nothing in the socialist ethic to condemn such action.

Private Ownership

The right of private ownership is based on the eighth commandment, "Thou shalt not steal." According to the Westminster Shorter Catechism, this commandment requires "the lawful procuring and furthering the wealth and outward estate of ourselves and others." The commandment forbids "whatsoever doth or may unjustly hinder our own or our neighbor's wealth or outward estate." The eighth commandment "means that the Bible countenances private property—for if a thing is not owned in the first place it can hardly be stolen."[9]

Harold Lindsell, in the course of explicating the hatred of socialist intellectuals for private property, unmasks the latent hypocrisy usually present. He observes that "ideas are property too. Professors who write books to expound their ideas secure copyrights which protect their words against plagiarism. *Das Kapital* by Karl Marx was protected by copyright! The simple truth is that socialists consistently violate their basic premise about private property in areas such as this so that they may profit from their labors!"[10]

The ninth commandment forbids lying. The whole idea of a free market implies that the parties to this voluntary exchange will not deceive each other. The doctrine of the harmony of interests in freedom largely depends for its working upon substantial voluntary compliance with this command.

Lying is an inescapable concomitant of socialism. The socialists must forever condemn profits, for instance, and the profit motive. But the truth is, socialist nations are just as profit-minded as are capitalist nations. The difference: In capitalist nations the individual reaps the profits and decides how they will be used; in Socialist nations the state reaps the profits and determines what to do with them. So lying, even about its basic tenets, is crucial to socialism.

The tenth commandment, "Thou shalt not covet," "means that it is sinful even to contemplate the seizure of another man's goods—which is something which Socialists, whether Christians or otherwise, have never managed to explain away."[11] Coveting is a root of all social evil.

How Envy Destroys

Envy, a central aspect of covetousness, involves not only the desire to possess another's property, but also—and perhaps more heinous—the desire to see another's wealth or station reduced to the level of one's own. "Envy is ineluctable, implacable and irreconcilable, is irritated by the slightest differences, is independent of the degree of inequality, appears in its worst form in social proximity or among near relations, provides the dynamic for every social revolution, yet cannot of itself produce any kind of coherent revolutionary programme."[12]

Rushdoony points out that the tenth commandment "forbids the expropriation by fraud or deceit of that which belongs to our neighbor. The tenth commandment therefore does sum up commandments six through nine and gives them an additional perspective. The other commandments deal with obviously illegal acts, i.e., clear-cut violations of law. The tenth commandment can be broken within these laws." This law forbidding dishonest gain "is directed by God, not merely to the individual, but to the state and all institutions. The state can be and often is as guilty as are any individuals, and the state is often used as the legal means whereby others are defrauded of their possessions."[13] Socialism, through its employment of the police powers of the state for the purpose of expropriating the wealth of producers to transfer to nonproducers, is a form of institutionalized envy.

Christ summarized the second table of the law like this: "Thou shalt love thy neighbor as thyself." Shenfield observes that we usually understand the command to love our neighbor "to mean to heal the sick, to succor the poor, to relieve human distress of all kinds, and the like." He then suggests that whatever else such love means, "It must mean that one wishes one's neighbor to have what one most values for oneself. . . ." In the final analysis, "what we want above all for ourselves, and which therefore we must accord to our neighbor, is freedom to pursue our own purposes."[14]

Our conclusion, then, is that the claim that capitalism is inherently immoral is not only false, but the exact opposite of the truth. Only the much-maligned capitalism, of all contemporary forms of economic organization, is founded upon and consistent with an immutable moral foundation.

---

1. Owen Chadwick, *The Secularization* of *the European Mind in the Nineteenth Century* (Cambridge University Press, 1975), p. 64.
2. Michael Novak, *The Spirit of Democratic Capitalism* (New York: Simon & Schuster, 1982), p. 262.
3. Arthur Shenfield, "Capitalism Under the Tests of Ethics," *Imprimis*, Vol. 10, No. 12, December 1981, pp. 1–2, 5.
4. Paul Johnson, *Enemies of Society* (New York: Atheneum, 1977), p. 191.
5. All quotations from Roepke are found in "The Moral Necessity of Economic Freedom," Intercollegiate Studies Institute, Inc., ISI Brief Essay Series, No. 1. Reprinted by permission from *Christian Economics*.
6. R. J. Rushdoony, *The Institutes of Biblical Law* (Nutley, N.J.: The Craig Press, 1973), p. 181.
7. John Chamberlain, *The Roots of Capitalism* (Princeton, N.J.: D. Van Nostrand Company, Inc., 1965), p. 46.
8. Gary North, "The Yoke of Co-operative Service," *Chalcedon Report*, No. 123, November 1975.
9. Chamberlain, *op. cit.*, p. 46.

10. Harold Lindsell, *Free Enterprise* (Wheaton, Ill.: Tyndale House Publishers, Inc., 1982), pp. 52–53.
11. Chamberlain, *op. cit.*, p. 46.
12. Helmut Schoeck, *Envy* (New York: Harcourt, Brace & World, Inc., 1970), p. 247.
13. Rushdoony, *op. cit.*, pp. 634–5.
14. Shenfield, *op. cit.*, p. 6.

The Morality of Capitalism

by E. Barry Asmus and
Donald B. Billings

A powerful and factual case has been made for the remarkable and unprecedented economic progress which inevitably follows the adoption of competitive capitalism and its central institutions of private property and voluntary social arrangements. Even Karl Marx, in the *Communist Manifesto,* pronounced capitalism a great "engine of growth." Undeniably, however, the market system of capitalism continues to be viewed as materialistic, ethically unjust, and consequently immoral by great numbers of people all over the world. This view is especially strong among the majority of so-called intellectuals.

Never mind the historical fact that systems other than capitalism trample freedoms, spawn totalitarian political regimes, reduce opportunity, and make a mockery of economic efficiency. Despite the evidence that central planning and economic equality lead to government intervention in private actions, and often ruthless dictatorship, the committed socialist of the left or right nevertheless believes that a small dose of socialism will one day glorify the human situation.

Interestingly, an increasing number of America's intellectual elite, known for their belief in "the mixed economy," "the middle way" or "economic democracy," are emerging from the socialist closet. They either admit to being socialists or, at the very least, are expressing preferences for an institutional mix other than free markets. Motives aside, their contention is that capitalism is inherently unfair. Without a moral basis, say the critics, the private property, free-market system could never be compassionate.

In the past, defenders of competitive capitalism have been just as

---

Dr. Asmus is senior economist for the National Center for Policy Analysis and a national speaker based in Phoenix, Arizona. Dr. Billings formerly taught college-level economics and now is a banking consultant in the Pacific Northwest.

This article, which appeared in the September 1985 issue of *The Freeman*, is taken from their book, *Crossroads: The Great American Experiment,* published in 1984 by University Press of America. Reprinted by permission of the publisher.

guilty as anyone for perpetuating this wrong-headed view. They have literally spent thousands of hours extolling the virtues of the efficiency of capitalism, free markets, and of the socially useful information generated by prices, wages, interest rates, profits, and losses. Pontificating on the efficiency aspects of capitalism, its supporters have failed to devote enough time and attention to the morality of the system. If the case for the morality of capitalism is not made, either through comparisons to its real world alternatives or on the basis of principle, then the probability of the great American experiment surviving is slim indeed.

The Moral Case for Capitalism

In fact, it should be clear that the most important part of the case for economic freedom is not its vaunted economic efficiency nor its dramatic success in promoting economic wealth and well-being, but rather that capitalism is consistent with certain fundamental moral principles of life itself. These are principles that respect the dignity and individuality of each person and that don't try to manipulate people as objects but recognize a person's rights and values. They seek to use persuasion and voluntary exchange rather than coercion and force. Competitive capitalism thrives on the non-aggression principle of human freedom.

The requirement that transactions in the private property, market order must be voluntary guarantees that the moral and physical autonomy of persons is protected from violent attack by others. Force is inadmissible in human relationships under a regime of capitalism. Personal freedom, and therefore economic and political freedom, is not "ethically indifferent," but a necessary condition of morality. Violence or the use of force against other individuals, which necessarily denies the most fundamental character of human freedom, the safety of persons and their property, is inconsistent with a moral order. The moral life requires that individuals act and make choices free of external intimidation and coercion. Friedrich Hayek reminds us of certain fundamental conditions of the moral life: "It is only where the individual has choice, and its inherent responsibility, that he has occasion to affirm existing values, to contribute to their further growth, and to earn moral merit." Moral choice presumes the necessary freedom to exercise our responsibilities.

The free market system, in which only voluntary and mutually beneficial exchange is permitted, is consistent with freedom-of-choice, and, therefore, offers the greatest potentiality for a moral order in which the integrity of the individual conscience is respected. Hayek, in a warning to us about the undesirable consequences of a planned, socialist order, wrote in *The Road to Serfdom* that only:

> . . . where we ourselves are responsible for our own interest . . . has our decision moral value. Freedom to order our own conduct in the sphere where material circumstances force a choice upon us, and responsibility for the arrangement of our own life according to our own conscience, is the air in which alone moral sense grows and in which moral values are daily recreated in the free decision of the individual. Responsibility . . . to bear the consequences of one's own decisions [is] the very essence of any morals which deserve the name.

It is frequently asserted that the materialistic character of capitalism is at the very least amoral. However, it is surely an error to blame a social system for being too concerned with material things simply because the individuals in that system remain free to decide for themselves those goals which are to be pursued.

The practice of blaming capitalism for being materialistic is to miss the point. Most would agree that capitalism does have a record of organizing resources efficiently. It is also important to note that very few people go hungry under this system. In comparison, socialism fails on both counts. Yet, material abundance is admittedly but *one* of the positive attributes of living. In most societies with which we are familiar, it is only a minority who are not concerned with economic growth and material gain. As much or even more than market economies, socialist nations of both the left and right place most of their emphasis on economic growth, industrial production, and personal sacrifice in the pursuit of material ends.

Unfortunately, the people in planned societies who are not materially oriented, those, for example, who might want to pursue the life of a recluse, take a vow of poverty, or seek some spiritual end, are persecuted. Freedom, it seems, is more important to the minority of those who do not have material objectives than it is to those who do. Only in a decentralized, pluralistic, private property order can inalienable rights of these persons who are different be secure. But whatever the goals of individuals, whether virtuous, materialistic, or whatever, the market still seems to be the most humane way mankind has found for dealing with the economic problems of scarcity and the efficient allocation of resources.

The Humane Effects of Freedom

One of the great advantages of a social system characterized by social cooperation through mutually beneficial exchange is the opportunity and scope for sympathy, beneficence, and human friendships. Indeed, the libertarian scholar Murray Rothbard reminds us that ". . . it is far more likely that feelings of friendship and communion are the effects of a regime of contractual social cooperation rather than the cause." Each individual has a uniqueness. In that sense, it is difficult for anyone else to say what will or will not lead to another's fulfillment.

Naturally, when we disagree with a person's actions, there exists the tendency to save that person from himself. Fortunately, capitalism tends to favor those who respect the sanctity of the other person's autonomy because of the respect for and enforcement of private property rights. The deterioration in many socially useful conventions, and the decay of morality which people have felt in recent years, are partially the result of our shift in thinking from personal to social responsibility. As persons are told their behavior and circumstances are not their fault, behavior is modified, society is indicted, and government is viewed as the only institution capable of solving the problem.

The work ethic, encouraged by the institution of private property, represents an important source of moral responsibility as well as a continuous reminder that our actions always entail costs. The essential ingredients of a free market order define a set of social institutions which encourage mutual respect for each and every individual. In contrast with all other economic systems, competitive capitalism operates on a set of rules which encourages mutual respect for persons with whom we interact.

The processes by which we satisfy material wants through social cooperation do not exhaust the goals which individuals might hope to achieve. The search for personal happiness and inner peace, for example, must be found within the individual alone. Nevertheless, mankind's social relationships are generally far more peaceful under a system of private property and free trade. The period between the Napoleonic Wars and World War I, the heyday of competitive capitalism, represented a century relatively free of the brutality of war. Furthermore, competitive capitalism was the first social system in human history to direct an individual's desire to become rich by peacefully supplying greater quantities of goods and services for other human beings.

The market process has been especially productive in providing greater abundance for the working class and the poor. Unfortunately, the alternative to serving other people's wants through voluntary exchange is to try to control their lives through the use of force. Wherever socialism has prevailed, it has invariably meant lower living standards for most people, and the subjugation of the many by the privileged few. A socialist country of the left or right, with few if any exceptions, means a totalitarian political regime in which other civil and human freedoms disappear and a form of slavery ensues.

Capitalism and Religion

The case for morality and justice of the system of capitalism rests on the intimate and complementary connection between private property and voluntary arrangements, and the sovereignty of the individual over his own life. We tend to take the concept of individuality for granted, but in reality, this concern and interest for the individual came into its own only with the rise of capitalism. In fact, the market system, far from dehumanizing man, finally allowed him to assume his full individuality. The individual conscience and its potential for discerning right and wrong, which was recognized during the early Christian period, came to full fruition under the system of competitive capitalism.

The "dawn of conscience," that point in history in which individuals were first argued to be morally free and, therefore, responsible for their actions, first appeared in Egypt and was later borrowed and developed by the Jews. Later Jesus and the Apostle Paul outlined a view which recognized the unique personality of each human being. Essentially, this account represented an individualistic view of mankind which maintained that the individual's soul is the most important thing about him. Christianity provided an environment in which individuals, in order to gain salvation, made choices from a position of free will.

Not only did the church discover that individual souls were worth saving, but Christianity also implanted the concept of the "rule of law." This attention to the notion of legality also proved to be important in the development of the idea of freehold property and the land deed in the Western world. Admittedly, these contributions were largely to protect the church and its institutions and property from the power of the secular State. But over time, the principles of the "rule of law," and the private ownership of property were progressively expanded to the relationships between individuals. There is a distinct and important connection between the Judeo-Christian morality and a free-market economy. This relationship rests on the established view of the central importance of the individual in the analysis of social relationships.

The system of free and open markets is most conducive to the perfection, or at least improvement, of man's free will, which tends to generate and make moral behavior possible. One can learn correct behavior only if one is allowed to make mistakes and, hopefully, to learn from them. After all, one possible consequence of making a mistake is wisdom. Unfortunately, the larger the influence of government in people's lives, the less opportunity there exists for an unhindered and free exercise of a person's moral faculties.

Society itself cannot be moral or immoral; only individuals are moral agents. Following the argument developed by Arthur Shenfield, it would appear that in an economic system, ". . . if its essential characteristics on balance positively nurture or reinforce moral or immoral individual behavior, [then] . . . it is a moral or immoral system in its effects." Competitive capitalism, under the rule of law, positively nurtures moral behavior and, therefore, can be moral in its effects. Where justly acquired property rights are defended, and where contracts are enforced, and where the rule of law applies, then "the voluntary nature of capitalist transactions propels us into respect for others."

Morality and Personal Taste

It is, of course, impossible to argue that a system of competitive capitalism will always produce values and behavior of which we would individually approve. However, it is important that we tolerate the "undefendable," undesirable, or annoying behavior of others as long as it is peaceful. An individual should not violate what the nineteenth-century sociologist Herbert Spencer called his "law of equal freedom," which states that ". . . every man has freedom to do all that he wills, provided he infringes not the equal freedom of any other man." Consequently, peaceful, non-violent human action is not a crime. Those who really believe in freedom must oppose coercive acts which would deny the possibility of a moral life by preventing that freedom of choice which morality requires. Given the uniqueness of individuals and the varied goals they pursue, we must allow actions which, while permissible in a free society, are offensive to personal tastes.

Lysander Spooner, a great and passionate defender of individual liberty during the nineteenth century, recognized an important distinction: the criminal and/or violent invasion of one's person or property is different in kind from behavior, ". . . whilst perhaps immoral in some broader sense, must be allowed to flourish, and even be given the full protection of the law." Morality is impossible unless one has the freedom to choose between alternative courses of action without external coercion. It was the great humanitarian Albert Schweitzer who said that civilization can only revive when there shall come into being a number of individuals who would develop a new tone of mind, independent of and in opposition to, the prevalent one among the crowd—a point of view which gradually wins influence over the collective mind and in that manner determines its character.

Only a movement grounded in a revised ethical perspective can rescue us from this relentless slide into collectivism. Necessarily, the revised moral point of view will come into existence *only by individual choice*. Once again, we encounter the proposition that it is the free market economic system of private property and voluntary exchange which maximizes the *potential* for leading a moral life.

The effects and results of the competitive process under capitalism are generally consistent with a moral order, but even when they are not it is still terribly important to oppose coercive restrictions of human behavior unless they violate the law of equal freedom. Diverse lifestyles and unique opinions represent one of the main arguments for human liberty. It is under a system of private property and free markets where sometimes annoying or even obnoxious activities are protected by the laws of a free society.

Morality and Its Alternatives

In summary, the system of institutional arrangements called "capitalism," a disparaging reference for many people, is unquestionably more consistent with morality and justice in our social arrangements than any alternative set of social institutions presently conceivable to us. The obviously immoral character of the socialist dictatorships in Poland, Cuba, East Germany, the People's Republic of China, the Soviet Union, the Ayatollah's Iran, and the right-wing fascist dictatorships in countries like Argentina and Chile,where the most elementary human freedoms are suppressed, and where millions of human beings have been murdered in the name of a new social order, documents the case for the free, open, and decentralized market system. [Ed. note: As of 1992, only Cuba and the People's Republic of China still fit the description.]

Poverty and brutality are repulsive. From any point of view, starving children must be viewed with anguish. We ask then, under what economic systems are the greatest number of people leading lives with sufficient food, self-chosen occupations, and the greatest degree of inward and outward independence? In which countries do individuals have the opportunity to be free, really *free*? Have the socialist countries delivered this choice, mobility, and independence? Or, in fact, is it best nurtured in an open market, private property, and limited government social order?

Within the Limits of Right

These questions have already been answered. The Soviet Union talked about "freedom" and "democracy," but they didn't seem to have much of an immigration problem. Communist East Germany, on the other hand, had to build massive steel and concrete walls and guard them continuously to prevent an exodus of their people. Even in the so-called "social democracies," the construction of peaceful and egalitarian systems is failing. In recent years the declining French economy, under a more intense Mitterrand brand of socialism, has been on international display. The myth of the Swedish utopia has been fully revealed for what it really is in *The New Totalitarians* by Roland Huntford.

The great French economist and social critic Frederic Bastiat, writing in the nineteenth century, captured what would be the desirable characteristics of a truly just and moral order. He asked an important question:

> . . . which countries contain the most peaceful, the most moral, and the happiest people? Those people are found in the countries where the law least interferes with private affairs; where the government is least felt; where the individual has the greatest scope, and free opinion the greatest influence; where the administrative powers are fewest and simplest; where taxes are lightest and most nearly equal; . . . where individuals and groups most actively assume their responsibilities, and, consequently, where morals of . . . human beings are constantly improving; where trade, assemblies, and associations are the least restricted; . . . where mankind most nearly follows its own natural inclinations; . . . in short, the happiest, most moral, and most peaceful people are those who most nearly follow this principle: Although mankind is not perfect, still, all hope rests upon the free and voluntary actions of persons within the limits of right; law or force is to be used for nothing except the administration of universal justice.

Understanding that the case we have made for the moral basis of capitalism requires further refinement, we defer to the wisdom of St. Augustine. He argued that material well-being does not necessarily bring better choices, a finer morality, or even more happiness. Referring to earth and the human predicament, he writes: "The things which the earthly city desires cannot justly be said to be evil, for it is itself, in its own kind, better than all other human goods. For it desires earthly peace for the sake of enjoying earthly goods. It is all right for men to seek these things, for they are good things, and without doubt, the gifts of God. But there is something better and that is the heavenly city which is secured by eternal victory and peace never ending." That kind of morality is between each person and his God. Salvation is quite another matter.

The Exciting Study of Freedom

Despite the arguments of Bastiat, Hayek, Shenfield, and others, a very interesting and important question remains to be asked.

Why has a system of social organization which has produced historically unprecedented increases in living standards in those countries where the principles were practiced, and which simultaneously did so much to reduce man's inhumanity to man during its ascendancy, come to have such a low standing in the minds of so many millions of people? Hayek is surely right when he insists that we must once again make the study of freedom an exciting intellectual issue. Not just for economic, philosophical, or historical reasons, but for the billions of people who, whether they know it or not, must faintly perceive that ideas do have consequences, and that their lives are bound to be affected dramatically by the scribblings of philosophers. "Liberty," said Alexis de Tocqueville, "cannot be established without morality, nor morality without faith."

If America is to survive, its indisputably modern elements must be conjoined with what Russell Kirk calls the "permanent things," and George Nash calls ". . . the spiritual things and the institutions that sustain them."

Ethics and Business

by Edmund A. Opitz

A few years ago there was an immensely popular television series, named after Dallas. The central character of this show was a powerful and unscrupulous businessman who got that way by climbing over the backs of rivals, manipulating politicians, and wheeling and dealing with shadowy figures on the fringes of the underworld. J. R. Ewing finally got in the way of a bullet, and for months this nation was racked by the question: "Who shot J.R.?" But the civilized man could only wonder why the trigger man waited so long!

Business and the businessman have had a bad press, almost uniformly. Do you remember the television show whose hero was a businessman? The show that portrayed this businessman as a person of integrity and vision, who labored long hours to produce a product that supplied a genuine need, which he marketed at prices people could afford? Who treated his employees with generosity and consideration, and his customers with unfailing courtesy? Who was a devoted family man, active in civic affairs, and a churchman? Who could recite Shakespeare by the yard, relaxed by listening to his fine collection of recorded symphony music, and could tell a Corot from a Monet? Do you remember that show? Perhaps it was a movie? Actually it was neither. Such a show was never produced; the subject is taboo, by today's mores.

The businessman has rarely if ever been treated fairly and accurately in drama or fiction. Is this because there are no men and women of superior intellect and high character in the world of business, industry, and trade? Not at all. Has the world of business no dramatic possibilities? Of course it has. But the fictional businessman invariably turns out to be the villain. There is a reason why this is so; the businessman is portrayed as a scoundrel because there is an almost universal bias against business on the part of

---

This paper was delivered at St. Mary's University, San Antonio, Texas. It originally appeared in the March 1993 issue of *The Freeman*.

novelists and dramatists. Businessmen do not get a fair shake because novelists and dramatists—with rare exceptions—have an ideological axe to grind.

This is the impression that emerges from our casual contact with the world of popular entertainment, the world of television, films, and fiction. This impression is confirmed in an unpretentious little volume by Ben Stein entitled *The View from Sunset Boulevard.* Stein interviewed a number of Hollywood writers and producers of television shows in order to find out how they viewed the various aspects of American life. If a visitor from England were to spend little time watching television, what image of America would he come away with? Stein deals with television's treatment of crime, the police, government, the army, the family, and other aspects of American life, including business. How do the people in Hollywood regard business? "One of the clearest messages of television," Stein writes, "is that businessmen are bad, evil people, and that big businessmen are the worst of all. . . the murderous, duplicitous, cynical businessman is about the only kind of businessman there is on TV adventure shows, just as the cunning, trickster businessman shares the stage with the pompous buffoon businessman in situation comedies." A well known producer, Stanley Kramer, sees business as "part of a very great power structure which wields enormous power over the people." And beyond that, Kramer implies, there is an "arrangement" between business and organized crime: "the Mafia is part of the entire corporate entity now."

The warped feelings of wealthy and talented Hollywood writers and producers did not spring into existence unaided; it is one of the calculated end results of an intense propaganda effort that has been hacking away at the roots of Western society since the middle of the last century—attacking its religious origin, its values, and what is perceived as the last bastion of the bourgeoisie, business. A scholarly work which meticulously researched this vast literature appeared in 1954, by Professor James Desmond Glover of the Harvard Business School, entitled *The Attack on Big Business.* Professor Glover writes: "In volumes upon volumes of testimony before Congressional committees, in popular novels, in learned treatises and textbooks, in poetry, in sermons, in opinions of Supreme Court justices, 'big business' and its works are seen as evil and attacked. The literature of criticism of 'big business,' and of the civilization it has done so much to bring into being, represents by now a perfectly staggering mass of material."

The Anti-Capitalistic Mentality

What is the rationale for this widespread antagonism toward the business system, otherwise known as capitalism? I don't profess to understand all the reasons for the anti-capitalistic mentality, but the root cause of the antipathy is surely the perception, the mistaken perception, that the relation between employer and employee is that of exploiter to victim. The employer may intend no harm, he may intend only good to those who work for him, but in the capitalistic mode of production—Karl Marx contended—the worker is denied the full fruits of his labor; a portion of every wage earner's product is garnisheed by his boss. To simplify Marxist theory, we might say that John Smith—who runs a machine in a shoe factory—punches the clock at eight o'clock in the morning and works till noon. During these four hours he produces six pairs of shoes, which represent his wage for the day. John Smith returns to his bench and works four more hours in the afternoon, but the shoes he produces during these four hours are expropriated by his employer.

This is a summary statement of the surplus value theory, otherwise known as Marx's exploitation theory. It is a central contention of Marxism that labor alone creates value, the value of a commodity being measured by the quantity of labor normally necessary to produce it. But if it is labor alone that creates value, the value created should belong exclusively to labor. It does not, however; the lion's share is grabbed by the employer while the real producer is paid only a subsistence wage.

This theory overlooks the role of tools and machinery in production. The tool user in this generation is many times more productive than his counterpart of a few generations ago. Why is this? His naked labor power is no greater than that of people over the ages. The enhanced productivity of labor today is due to the tools and machinery at the disposal of every one of us—and those tools are the fruits of the labor of earlier generations. If today's "worker" retained the full product of his individual effort, and only that, the poor fellow would starve.

A contemporary of Marx, the celebrated Austrian economist Eugen von Böhm-Bawerk, demolished the surplus value theory in a book entitled *Capital and Interest*, published in 1884, the year after Marx died. The demolition job has been repeated many times since the appearance of Böhm-Bawerk's great book, and the consensus of opinion among independent economists is that the surplus value theory does not hold water. The exploitation theory has great propaganda value, however, and it is used unthinkingly by those who are acting out a grudge against business, which, in their distorted vision, keeps the poor locked in their poverty in order that others might be rich.

Ben Stein, in the book mentioned earlier, records a portion of his conversation with television writer Bob Weiskopf:

"Q. Why are people poor in America?

"A. Because I don't think the system could function if everyone was well off.

"Q. What do you mean?

"A. I think you have to have poor people in a capitalist society.

"Q. Why?

"A. To exploit. The rich people can't exploit each other. Consequently they always exploit the poor."

It is not only Hollywood script writers who profess to believe that the rich get richer only by making the poor poorer. The coordinator of the National Council of Churches' Anti-Poverty Task Force asserts that, "Poverty would not continue to exist if those in power did not feel it was good for them." A moment's reflection will reveal this insulting accusation for the silly sentiment it is. We live in a commercial and manufacturing society. Our economy is featured by mass production, not only in factories but also in agriculture. The products of mass production flood our stores and supermarkets and showrooms, to be bought by the mass of consumers. Mass production cannot continue unless there is mass consumption; and the masses of people cannot consume the output of our mass production factories and fields unless they possess purchasing power—the money to buy the goods of their choice. To suggest that those who have goods and services to sell have some sinister interest in keeping their potential customers too poor to buy is sheer nonsense! If the president of General Motors wants to sell you a Cadillac or a Buick or a Chevrolet—which he does—then he wants you to be rich enough to buy. In the free economy, everyone has a stake in the economic well-being of every other person.

It is in the immediate interest of business and businessmen that the masses of people be well off; people who are poor are poor customers, and business cannot survive without customers. Business has no stake in poverty; but there is a class of people who do need the poor, who do have an interest in keeping them poor. Permit me, in a slight digression, to offer you a few words on this point by the celebrated economist Thomas Sowell: "To be blunt, the poor are a gold mine. By the time they are studied, advised, experimented with and administered, the poor have helped many a middle class liberal to achieve affluence with government money. The total amount of money the government spends on its 'anti-poverty' efforts is three times what would be required to lift every man, woman, and child in America above the poverty line by simply sending money to the poor."

Back now to the widespread animus against business, stemming from the false idea that labor is the sole source of value but is not allowed to keep what it produces. In the distorted vision of Karl Marx, business, industry, and trade—as these economic activities are organized in the free world—are intrinsically evil, and the businessman is a parasite and predator. Similar notions are entertained by many a man in the street who has never read a line of Marx, as well as by intellectuals who regard themselves as anti-Communists. Given this climate of opinion, the term "ethical businessman" is a contradiction in terms; it is the figure of speech known to English teachers as an oxymoron—a figure which juxtaposes incongruous terms like "virtuous thief" or "honest liar."

Now, if businessmen are involved in activities which are intrinsically crooked, evil by their very nature, then it is pointless to discuss the ethical situations of business or the moral dilemmas businessmen sometimes face. It would be like instructing a thief on how to rob banks honestly! So I propose to spend a few minutes trying to understand the nature of the economic activities that engage businessmen, while touching upon some of the values that are implicated in the production of goods and services.

All Are Sinners

You have a right to know the direction from which I am coming at you, to know my bias. I have examined the catalogue of sins of which businessmen are allegedly guilty, and Lo! they are the very same sins exhibited by people in every other walk of life. We all break the Commandments now and then, every one of us. Businessmen have no monopoly on sin. My mind goes back to a conversation I had several years ago with a professor of economics with years of teaching behind him, who had also served for many years as the academic dean of a prestigious midwestern college. He said to me, "You know, Ed, a thoroughly dishonest man can last a lot longer in teaching or preaching than as a used car salesman." There may be some hyperbole here, but my friend has a point. There are good and bad in all walks of life, and there are very few saints anywhere; but in the eyes of the law all are equal. The law should mete out justice upon the guilty party with impartiality. It should punish those who harass, steal, defraud, breach a contract, assault, or murder. This is the rule of law in action.

There is no justification for the assumption that all businessmen are evil people who must therefore be regulated, i.e., adjudged guilty until proven innocent. There is no more reason for regulating businessmen than for regulating clergymen or teachers!

Who Decides?

The free market economic system produces goods and services in abundance, and it rewards every participant according to his individual contribution—as his peers judge that contribution. "To the producer belongs the fruits of his toil," is an ancient bit of wisdom, as true now as when first uttered. The relation between an individual's effort and the eventual reward of his exertions is fairly clear in a simple situation like subsistence farming. You work by yourself, preparing the ground in the spring, seeding and tilling it, watering the furrows with your sweat during the heat of summer, reaping in the fall. The abundance of your harvest is directly traceable to your skills and the amount of work you put forth. The greater your effort the more ample your harvest—other things being equal. The harvest is your wage, and your wage in this instance is pretty much determined by your own skill and your own exertions; the more you put in the more you will take out. What you take out is your wage, the economic equivalent of your contribution.

How is your wage determined in a complex division of labor society such as ours? Justice still demands that every participant in the economy be rewarded according to his contribution to the productive process. But how shall we identify each individual's contribution in order to reward him commensurately? Economists from Adam Smith to Ludwig von Mises to F. A. Hayek and Milton Friedman have worked this question over and come up with an answer that is completely democratic and economically efficient, while encouraging every person in the full exercise of his lawful liberties. The answer provided by the economist is: Let the market decide what each person's contribution is worth and reward him accordingly. "The market" describes the process of social cooperation under the division of labor where free people specialize in a complex variety of tasks in anticipation of a consumer demand for the goods and services they produce—followed by multiple voluntary exchanges of these products in which persons give over something they value for whatever they value more. This market process will reward people unequally, but it will reward them equitably, compensating each person in a measure equal to his peers' evaluation of his services.

The eminent economist Frank H. Knight, founder of the Chicago School, put the matter in these words: "It is a proposition of elementary economics that ideal market competition will force entrepreneurs to pay every productive agent employed what his cooperation adds to the total, the difference between what it can be with him and what it would be without him. This is his own product in the only meaning the word can have where persons or their resources act jointly." In short, each person will get his fair share, defined as what others will voluntarily offer for his goods and services—provided there is general freedom.

Each one of us is judged by his peers; our offerings of goods and services are evaluated by consumers who give us what they think our offerings are worth to them, and not a penny more. This is a democratic judgment on the value of the products of our labor—one dollar, one vote—and it is made by consumers who are, as everyone knows, ignorant, venal, superstitious, neurotic, biased, and stupid. In other words, people just like us—because every one of us is a consumer! When it is a question of the wage we earn we are dependent on consumers, who couldn't care less that we are upright men of sterling character; their sole concern is: Do we have a product or service they want? If we do, they reward us handsomely. If we don't, it matters not that we have labored long and painfully over our brainchild; if the customers don't want it, we're stuck with it. This is consumer sovereignty.

Consumers run the free economy; producers cater to their demands. It's their show. What kind of a show do they put on? Not always a good one, I'm sorry to say. But I'll say one thing for consumer sovereignty: it sure beats the alternative.

Freedom to Excel and Fail

Freedom is a costly thing, and we cannot keep it unless we are willing to pay the price. It is required of each one of us that we firmly adhere to the processes of freedom, even when we can barely stand some of the products of freedom—the products being what people do when given their "druthers." The freer the society the more things people will do that we might find distasteful; this is one of the consequences of freedom, and we have to school ourselves to accept it. This we have learned to do in two important areas—freedom of the press and freedom of worship. We must learn to be equally tolerant in the areas of business, industry, and trade.

How fares the written word when the masses are relatively literate and free to pick their own reading material, where they themselves select the men and women who will do their writing for them? The highest paid writers may be those whose subliterary efforts jam the boob tube, some of whose opinions I quoted earlier. The magazines and newspapers of largest circulation may be those which cater to our prurient interests. Best-selling novels are forgotten by next year. But as much as anyone might deplore the decline of reading and the low estate of publishing—now that the press is free—no one with any sense would wish to add a Department of Censorship to the already overgrown government bureaucracy. To put the press under a Ministry of Information and Propaganda would be disastrous. Freedom of the press may give every idiocy a voice; authors may not reap a monetary reward commensurate with their literary talents; so be it, we say; it's the price we pay willingly for freedom of the press. Freedom merely allows the budding genius the elbow room he needs to live, and breathe, and write. And books of solid scholarly competence still appear regularly for the small audience which needs the nourishment only the word can provide. My mind goes back to an observation of Ralph Waldo Emerson: "There are not in the world at any one time more than a dozen persons who read and understand Plato:—never enough to pay for an edition of his works; yet to every generation these [works] come duly down, for the sake of those few persons. . . ."

Take the matter of religious liberty, the separation of church and state. In a free society people are not punished for belonging to the "wrong" church. They belong to the church of their own choice, or they belong to no church, as the case might be. In any event, the law pays no attention, so long as no injury is done to person or property. What happens when people are free in the area of religion? First of all, they mangle the phrase "separation of church and state" into my least favorite American shibboleth! Even people who should know better distort and misuse the phrase.

Then there are the so-called "electronic churches," the spellbinders who appear in television; there are the "hot gospellers" who dominate radio every Sunday morning; there are the cults in which people give over their souls to some figure of dubious charismatic allure; there is the new appeal of mystical imports from the exotic Orient; the occult flourishes, along with magic and superstition. And the mainline churches, in many instances, have subordinated theology to dubious economic and political theory. Church bodies support and help finance revolutionary and guerrilla activities. But is anyone campaigning to establish a government Department of Religion? Not to my knowledge. However much we may dislike certain manifestations of religion when belief is free, we shrug our shoulders and tolerate what we dislike as the price of religious liberty.

Some of these same considerations apply to the realm of business, industry, and trade, where, as H. L. Mencken once wryly observed: "Nobody ever went broke by underestimating the taste of the American public." This is all too obvious in what is called the entertainment industry. Here is a hyperkinetic young man, lacking in musical sense, who makes eight million dollars a year by howling and gyrating in public places. Here's another young man, gifted with a high musical I.Q. and years of study behind him. A handful of people appreciate his organ virtuosity and his sensitive interpretation of Bach. He earns a living as a bank teller, directs a choir, and gives an occasional free organ recital. Young people pay millions of dollars to hear the Rolling Stones, while the Boston Symphony has to pass the hat in order to survive. Is this fair? No. Is it a matter for political solution? That would be an even greater travesty of justice.

The Market Economy

Human beings everywhere have engaged in trade and barter. There is some specialization and a division of labor even among primitive people, with a consequent exchange of the fruits of specialization. The voluntary exchange of goods and services is the market in operation, and the market is everywhere. But the market does not spontaneously or automatically transform itself into the market economy; the market economy emerges only when the moral, political, and legal conditions are right. This occurred under the Whig philosophy of men like Edmund Burke and Adam Smith, Thomas Jefferson and James Madison. These men drew up a frame of government whose main purpose was to secure each person in his life, liberty, and property. This political idea of limited, constitutional government is grounded on the religious conviction that we are God's creatures, possessing immortal souls. The conviction that persons are sacred is politically translated into our Creator-endowed rights to "life, liberty, and the pursuit of happiness." Adam Smith referred to his "liberal plan of liberty, equality and justice," with the free market as the economic counterpart to political liberty. The rule of law replaces the arbitrary will of rulers and personal freedom expands. It is significant that *The Wealth of Nations* appeared in the same year as the Declaration of Independence.

The discipline of economics as a separate subject matter was almost non-existent prior to Adam Smith. Virtually starting from scratch, Smith created nearly the whole edifice of economics.

Adam Smith presupposed the legal framework of the Whig jurists, where the law would eliminate force from the marketplace, punish fraud, and enforce contracts. He also presupposed a high level of probity in the general population. Given these conditions, the market is self-starting and self-regulating; the buying habits of consumers guide producers, determining how the entrepreneur will decide to combine scarce resources for the maximum satisfaction of consumer needs. There will be a harmony in these diverse activities of millions of participants as if everything were directed by "an invisible hand." The market economy—dubbed "capitalism" by its enemies about a century after Smith—contained the promise of prosperity for the multitudes. These same masses composed a self-governing people. Political liberty expanded and people had lots of elbow room to pick and choose and plan their own lives.

The Declaration and the Constitution created the political frame for a people who aspired to the ideal of "liberty and justice for all." Political liberty assured freedom in economic transactions between employer and employee, seller and buyer. The work ethic was enshrined in America and wages doubled, redoubled, and doubled again during the nineteenth century—an eightfold increase in real wages. For the first time in history the masses glimpsed the possibility of pulling themselves out of poverty and creating new opportunities for their children. America's schools and churches sought to shore up the traditional value structure of our culture and to orient the newly enlarged popular freedom toward virtue. Their success, needless to say, was only partial.

Was there ugliness in American life? Of course there was. Freedom was misused; the scramble for wealth was sometimes pretty crass. The newly rich were vulgar; plunderers bought and sold politicians, and fortunes were scooped out of the public treasury—all in violation of Whig theory and free market economics. But you cannot blame capitalism for the miscreants who refuse to abide by its rules.

Despite the gray and black areas in our history, there was still open opportunity on these shores, in comparison to what was available in other parts of the globe. Thirty-three million people told us so by coming here as immigrants during the half century before World War I. They came because life here—although far from perfect—was far better for them than life elsewhere.

The business of America is not business. It never was. The business of America is individual liberty, with the law enforcing an even-handed justice among equal persons. When the law provides a free field and no favor—which was the original implication of *laissez faire*—the economic order is the free market.

The market economy does not carry any implication that business may act irresponsibly with impunity. If, for example, industrial wastes are disposed of in such a way that persons are injured or property damaged, the law should punish those responsible and offer redress to the injured party. If a seller misrepresents a product he is guilty of fraud and the buyer's injury should be redressed. If a businessman solicits and obtains a subsidy from government, or if government gives him monopolistic advantages over his competition enabling him to exact a higher price from his customers, he has forfeited his status as a businessman. A businessman as such has no power over anyone, his only leverage being the quality of his goods and the persuasiveness of his advertising. The businessman has the same rights and the same responsibilities as every other member of society, no more and no less.

Lord Acton's aphorism about power has been overquoted, but it is still terribly true. Power must be curbed if we will that people shall be free, and an independent economic order does put fetters on governmental power. People who control their own livelihood have little to fear from rulers; but political control of the economic life of a nation is totalitarian rule. The market economy curbs power in another way as well; it channels the activities of energetic, ambitious, and competitive personalities into the production of goods and services and away from politics. The rich in a free economy get that way because consumers appreciate the goods and services they offer; and if these few wish their descendants to enjoy this wealth the bulk of it must be invested in industries producing goods for the masses.

The End of Liberty

Let us give credit where credit is due; business, industry, and trade have made us into a prosperous nation. But our wealth has not made us a happy nation, or a contented one. We have proved once again—as if any further proof were needed—that prosperity and worldly success are, at best, a means to ends beyond themselves. Refine and improve a means as you will, it still remains only a means, needing a worthy end if it is to be meaningful. There is a discipline that deals with ends and goals, with the purposes that make life significant; it is called religion—though not everything bearing that label qualifies. But genuine Christianity is at a low ebb in the modern world; we have lost that vital contact with God and the moral law which energized our ancestors and made life for them an adventure in destiny. The decadence of Christianity is the root cause of the modern malaise; Plato argued two millennia ago that disorder in society is a reflection of disorder in the soul, that is, in our defective thinking and misguided loyalties. The work of renewal must begin here, with individual persons, and then go on to a restoration of the theological foundation necessary to a free society.

This is not the task of business, industry, and trade; the economic order has a more humble role to play. Business and the free economy beget a prosperous society which provides people the leisure they need to cultivate those goods which mark a high civilization: religion and worship, education and science, arts and crafts, conversation and play. These are the areas where people exercise their freedom most creatively, where they discover the goals proper to human life. Responsible freedom in the economic realm has the important role of supplying the indispensable means for these ends.

The Ethics of Affirmative Action

by Steven Yates

Affirmative action has troubled the American political landscape for over three decades. Sooner or later, every ethicist must confront the dilemmas it and a variety of closely related policies—multicultural education, diversity management, sensitivity training sessions—pose. The dilemmas themselves indeed seem acute. It is true, for example, that U.S. history reveals poor treatment of this country's minorities and its powerless. Native Americans were taken from their lands and forcibly relocated. Decades of enforced discrimination left blacks well behind whites politically and socio-economically. Women were denied the right to vote for years.

The 1950s saw the start of an extensive effort to repudiate discrimination and bring about equal opportunity. Then something went wrong. The struggle for genuine equal opportunity was lost amidst the growing clamor by an ever-increasing number of groups for special government favors. Equal opportunity laws, which initially rejected preferential policies, were replaced by affirmative action programs which could not be implemented without them.

Backers of affirmative action argued that blacks and other victims of past discrimination were so far behind in the economic race that without preferential treatment, equal opportunity would never be more than a high-sounding phrase. Thus race-conscious policies emerged with a vengeance. Employers had to keep voluminous records on the race, gender, ethnic heritage, and religious background of prospective employees so they could prove they had not discriminated against those designated by the government as victims. Government agencies expanded their reach to oversee implementation. Those found not in compliance, even innocently, sometimes saw their businesses imperiled.[1]

White males started chafing at reverse discrimination right

Dr. Yates is a Bradley Visiting Fellow, Center for Economic Personalism, at The Acton Institute for the Study of Religion and Liberty. He is also the author of *Civil Wrongs: What Went Wrong With Affirmative Action* (San Francisco: ICS Press, 1994). This article originally appeared in the July 1994 issue of *The Freeman*.

away. Well-known cases such as *Bakke* and *Weber* resolved little, though, and future litigation seems inevitable. Meanwhile, special programs of all varieties not only failed to help the vast majority of those in targeted groups but left them worse off than before; the primary beneficiaries of affirmative action, after all, have not been the economically disadvantaged blacks and Native Americans, but middle- and upper-class women. The welfare state, another legacy of the 1960s, has now produced second- and third-generation dependents with no marketable skills and no incentive to acquire them. Victimology has become the country's largest growth industry—after government, of course.[2]

The affirmative action umbrella now covers roughly two thirds of the country's population, with the disabled and homosexuals the most recent entrants. Tensions between groups are at an all-time high, with skirmishes occurring constantly. The prevailing philosophy of multiculturalism which now underwrites much discussion of race, ethnicity, and gender has fueled division by emphasizing differences between groups.

What ought to concern the ethicist is the prevailing response to these problems. Instead of serious soul-searching and re-examination, an ambience of disinformation, concealment, and, when needed, outright dishonesty, has protected affirmative action and its kin for years. Begin with language. *Equal opportunity* clearly does not mean equal opportunity but preferences for some at the expense of others. Newspeak surrounds preferential policies with terms like *inclusion, celebrating diversity*, and *sensitivity*. Claims that affirmative action has sometimes forced businesses and entire industries to set quotas and hire by race and gender meet with belligerent denial, along with insinuations that only racists and sexists would make such charges. This tactic serves a very specific purpose: many white males, even those in positions of authority, will not question affirmative action for fear of being labeled racists. Finally, today's "sensitivity training" seems intended to inculcate in the white male who is turned down for a job or a promotion in favor of a less qualified woman or minority that, as a member of the oppressor group, he had it coming!

If affirmative action had been the boon to women and minorities its advocates claim, I doubt there would be much debate. Its benefits would be evident to everyone. What do we see instead?

We see growing populations of minorities who lack the basic skills necessary for economic advancement, and are actually slipping backward. We see an educational system which seems powerless to do anything, and rationalizes its own failings with doctrines which make achievement as well as experience a group-specific notion. In the view multiculturalists espouse, schools should give minority groups "self-esteem" instead of knowledge and marketable skills. Sometimes this means rewriting their histories to invent "achievements." Afrocentrism is the best example, with its claims that the Egyptians were black, that the Greeks stole their culture from Africa (the real origin of civilization), and that two thousand years of racism has suppressed the truth.[3] Radical feminism, the noisy stepchild of affirmative action for women, is also shot through with bizarre claims about sex and rape, our pornography-driven culture, and the universal victimization of women by "patriarchal society." The war against "sexual harassment" has created a climate in which men are guilty if charged.[4]

Clearly, we are on a downward spiral. Writers all across the political spectrum have observed that this balkanizing trend threatens not only basic Constitutional rights (such as First Amendment free speech protections) but the very fabric of representative democracy. Is there a better way? I think so. It's called the free market.

If transactions are voluntary and not coerced, businesses and other organizations will be free to hire according to their needs. This right will be *recognized* and *protected* by government. If personal responsibility is a central value, employers will *not* simply indulge base prejudicies or personal whims. Rather, business necessity—the necessity to remain as competitive as possible—will require employers to "cast their nets as widely as possible" and attempt to hire the best employees. A free market will ensure that information is available where qualified members of minority groups who are alert and seeking new opportunities will see it. In this sense, what has sometimes been called "weak" affirmative action will be permitted to continue on a *voluntary basis* among those who wish to continue it. As a voluntary enterprise, it may take a variety of forms which have the potential to address and solve the problems that coercive, government-driven affirmative action has been unable to touch, and without creating the dilemmas and rifts that coercive affirmative action has created.[5] Moreover, under conditions of genuine liberty, minorities will be freed from many constraints which have held them back: high taxes, licensure laws, zoning ordinances, etc.[6]

A question is in order. Given the freedom to do otherwise, will businesses and other institutions actually reach out to minorities? The mistrust evident in the question is actually misplaced. A recent study has shown that bigotry and prejudice are no longer considered acceptable to a majority of educated people.[7] *Education* has been and will continue to be the key. We should emphasize that racism is unfair to individuals whether directed by whites against blacks, or by blacks against whites. It is, in fact, a form of collectivism, and embodies its defects and follies in a particularly virulent form. Our tradition of individualism got rid of slavery. This tradition is still our best hope of keeping racism at bay.

At present, though, *coercion*, not *education*, is the norm. The proportioning of peoples by force is driving them apart rather than bringing them together. A new separation is loose in our society, fueled by the multiculturalist emphasis on how peoples differ instead of what they have in common.

Members of minority groups (and women) must be willing to question the dominant tendencies in what passes for education today. They need especially to question the collectivism and relativism inherent in multiculturalism, and affirm the values of liberty, responsibility, achievement, and toleration as values which hold universally, independently of race and gender. Then they will be motivated to obtain the skills they need to be employable, or to become entrepreneurs. This need not mean giving up a cultural or ethnic heritage but rather making an effort to preserve it in ways that don't undermine their capacity to prosper in a free society.

To sum up, government programs can never allocate skills where they are most needed. Lest the whole concept of "voluntary affirmative action" seem to place too much trust in human goodness, it is important to remember that government is the institution most responsible for the conditions minorities face. Slavery had foes as far back as the Revolutionary War, but continued under the support of government. Government instituted Jim Crow laws and involuntary segregation. Then, in our century, it passed minimum wage and licensure laws which effectively priced blacks out of the marketplace and created impassable barriers to their entry into many professions. Coercive preferential programs amount to government efforts to solve problems the government created in the first place—rather like using gasoline in an attempt to put out a fire.

For peaceful affirmative action to replace coercive affirmative action, though, criticisms by white males such as myself probably won't be enough. Women and minorities themselves must recognize that efforts by government to "help" them have proven futile. This means repudiating much of their current leadership. Fortunately, we have already seen the beginnings of such a trend in the writings of such black intellectuals as Thomas Sowell, Walter Williams, and Glenn Loury.[8] If the facts presented here and in countless other places can be shouted from the rooftops long enough, there may yet be hope for general economic advancement and intergroup peace in America.

---

1. Consider, for example, what happened to the tiny Daniel Lamp Company in Chicago. In 1989 the EEOC filed suit against Daniel Lamp and forced its owner, entrepreneur Mike Welbel, to pay over $130,000 to compensate alleged victims of racial discrimination in which the only evidence was the absence of an officially approved statistical ration. See my *Civil Wrongs,* chapter 1, for details.
2. See Charles J. Sykes, *A Nation of Victims* (New York: St. Martin's Press, 1992).
3. See for example Martin Bernal, *Black Athena* (New Brunswick, N.J.: Rutgers University Press, 1991).
4. For the latest account see Richard Bernstein, "Guilty If Charged," *New York Review of Books*, January 13, 1994, pp. 11–14.
5. Cf. Richard A. Epstein, *Forbidden Grounds: The Case Against Employment Discrimination Laws* (Cambridge: Harvard University Press, 1992).
6. For the best available account of these restrictions see Walter Williams, *The State Against Blacks* (New York: McGraw-Hill, 1982). Cf. also S. David Young, *The Rule of Experts* (Washington: The Cato Institute, 1987) ch. 12, for the effects of licensure on minorities and the poor.
7. For some statistics on white attitudes toward blacks see Paul M. Sniderman and Thomas Piazza *The Scar of Race* (Cambridge: Belknap Press of Harvard University Press, 1993).
8. For a good recent survey of "the new black vanguard" see Joseph G. Conti and Brad Stetson, *Challenging the Civil Rights Establishment: Profiles of a New Black Vanguard* (Westport, Conn.: Praeger Books, 1993).

The Immorality of Government-Mandated Health Care

by Paul A. Cleveland

As America's politicians debate the issue of health-care reform, one element seems strangely missing from their deliberations: the question of the morality of government-mandated health insurance. Is it moral for government to institute such insurance or to force employers to provide it? The current debate assumes that it is. Discussion has centered primarily on how far coverage can be extended, with no effort to defend the *morality* of mandated coverage.

To examine the morality of the proposed health reform we must ask the following questions: What is the role of government and what are its moral bounds? Also, how do these bounds apply to the current health-care reform debate? If, in this examination, it is discovered that government has no proper authority to insure the availability of goods and services generally, then all health-care reform proposals seeking to establish the provision of health insurance should be rejected.

The uncritical acceptance of the proposition that a major purpose of government is to insure the provision of some goods or services is related to another popularly held proposition. That notion, either conscious or unconscious, is that government can miraculously generate resources to provide for people's needs. But, how is that possible? Can government actually create material prosperity where none existed beforehand? Can it cause by fiat an increase in the number and kinds of products produced without harm? It should be self-evident that the answer to these questions is no. Government cannot create by mandate. It relies on its power of taxation and coercion to provide material benefits to selected citizens. In order for it to provide some benefit for an individual it must impose a cost of equal or greater value either on that individual or on someone else. Nevertheless, the mythical concept that

---

Dr. Cleveland is professor of economics and finance at Birmingham-Southern College in Alabama. This article originally appeared in the November 1994 issue of *The Freeman*.

government can provide cost-free benefits continues largely on the basis of wishful thinking and covetousness.

No Consumption Without Production

In reality there is no effortless production of anything. We can only consume that which is produced by the sweat of someone's brow. Furthermore, our government was not primarily instituted for the purpose of production. Its primary role with respect to the economy is to punish people who use force and deceit for their own gain. History is testimony to the extent to which some individuals will inflict pain and hardship on others in order to obtain what they desire. Thus government's primary role as an institution is to thwart this behavior by punishing the perpetrators of injustice. To that end, government uses force. Citizens are required to pay taxes to support the police function of government since society benefits from the ensuing order and peace which allow for civil relations among people.

Regrettably, this same force can be put to illegitimate ends. This occurs when the government begins to play favorites among the citizens by extending benefits to some while confiscating property or curbing the rights of others. The most obvious contemporary cases revolve around the many welfare programs established by the government. Benefits are extended to some by taxing away income from others. The costs of such benefits always exceed the costs of purchasing the benefits directly because of the bureaucratic overhead needed to administer the programs. Current health-care reform plans follow the same approach. Therefore, the question of the morality of any government provision of health care, or of mandated health insurance, can only be resolved by considering whether or not government redistribution of wealth is justified.

Do the Ends Justify the Means?

It is tempting to say that the ends aimed for are good and argue, therefore, that such government action is good. After all, what decent person would not desire to see some basic provision of food, clothing, or needed medical care provided for all those who could not pay? But to conclude that government intervention is good on this basis is to argue that the ends justify the means. The ends, in and of themselves, are not a sufficient reason for concluding that government provision of goods and services is just.

I recently had a conversation with a fellow professor about the health-care situation. My colleague expressed the common view. She argued that adequate health care is a right, "because we are human." But such a statement begs the question: How does being human, in and of itself, generate any rights? It is clear that being human alone cannot justify any rights for humans. David Hume once noted that "the rules of morality are not the conclusions of our reason." Therefore, if we carry Hume's statement to its logical conclusion, we must conclude that if any human rights exist, they exist only as they have been endowed. Thus rights must be defined apart from ourselves. Ultimately, they must be defined by the One who has the power of being in and of Himself, since He alone is in a position to establish such license. We are then dependent upon His proclamation of right and wrong to discern the rights of the individual. Apart from such an endowment, there are no rights! This view was expressed in the Declaration of Independence as well as many other writings and documents of the time.

Rights of Individuals

What are an individual's rights? As expressed in the Declaration, the individual is endowed with the right to life, liberty, and pursuit of happiness. These rights allow each individual to use his talents and his property freely to the ends he personally has in mind so long as he does not violate the rights of others. In this context, people can voluntarily interact and trade with others on mutually agreeable terms to further their own interests.

The Judeo-Christian heritage substantially affirms this understanding of individual rights. The Bible requires its reader to respect the property rights of others. "Thou shall not steal,"[1] and, "Cursed is the man who moves his neighbor's boundary stone,"[2] are its admonishments. In other places the Scriptures encourage hard work and honest dealings with others. Taken as a whole, the Bible prohibits the use of force to obtain what we wish to consume for ourselves. But this is exactly what transpires when government mandates a plan to provide health-care services to everyone! As already shown, the government by definition employs force. It is a coercive institution. Thus when government begins the process of providing, or mandating the provision of, goods and services in society, it ceases to perform its primary function of thwarting and punishing wrongdoers and actually begins to participate in the very plunder that it was supposed to stop. By using force to take from one person in order to give to another, it is involved in stealing.

Why has government more and more compromised its position by engaging in legal plunder when it is clear that such action is wrong? There are two reasons.[3] The first is selfishness. People would rather have someone else pay for their consumption than work hard and purchase things for themselves. This is as true for health care as it is for any other consumable. This was demonstrated during the last presidential campaign when a man phoned a radio talk show. Bill Clinton was well ahead of George Bush in the polls and he had promised to bring about government-mandated universal health insurance. To this situation the man proclaimed, "I can't wait 'til Bill Clinton is elected president and gets his health-care reform through Congress. Then I won't have to pray to God that my children don't get sick."

The caller had no intention of revealing his true character that day; but he did. In his proclamation we find a deeper problem. It is not that he lacks health insurance or that he cannot afford medical care. The real problem is that he does not want to pay for it himself. Rather, he wants someone else to pay, not as a matter of mercy shown to him, but as a matter of coercive force. Selfishness which leads to systematic thievery will destroy a nation. A nation can survive and prosper when there are a few thieves, but as more people leave productive endeavors to participate in government largess, production wanes and economic hardships increase. This is the inevitable outcome of all government schemes aimed at providing some benefit for some citizens at the expense of others.

The second is perhaps the most pervasive reason for the government's drift toward promoting welfare programs in general, and for its current consideration of mandating the provision of universal health insurance. Americans have traditionally been compassionate. Generosity for those in need has been a hallmark feature of the American experience. Private charities, churches, nonprofit organizations, and the volunteerism associated with them have been a salient feature of our culture. Stated simply, the American people have a passion for helping out those in need. This spirit is the reason why most of our hospitals developed as non-profit institutions. Yet it is this very passion which threatens to undermine the fabric of our society when charity is pursued by way of governmental mandate.

It is not hard to see how this situation can arise. At any given point in time, the available resources to meet our ends are always limited. That is, we can always imagine a better circumstance than the one we are presently in. If this is true for individuals, how much more true is it for voluntary groups seeking to do good? It is, therefore, easy to see the temptation facing people who desire to show mercy and compassion toward others: to use voluntary contributions to lobby for government action rather than devoting them directly to the cause in mind. If the efforts are successful, the organization can tap into the much larger pool of resources available in the public treasury to promote their cause. If passion for the cause blurs their vision, then they may well use government force and, as a result, inflict harm upon the neighbors they aim to help. Such is the state of American "do-goodism" in the twentieth century—coercive charity.

This movement has been greatly aided by the religious community. One cannot read the Bible for long without realizing that it calls its followers to show mercy and compassion toward others. As a result, well-meaning people have often pushed for government intervention because they see the public treasury as the only institution which has a pool of funds large enough to meet the need. However, the Bible never suggests that the government is the means through which mercy is to be shown. Actually, the evidence indicates that such action is more than inappropriate. When Satan offered to place Jesus in political control of the kingdoms of the earth, Jesus rejected the offer arguing that it was sin to have other gods above God.[4] Jesus understood that mercy and compassion are voluntary responses motivated by love and that no government is capable of forcing people to love their neighbors. He understood that any such attempts were nothing more than a false image intended to mimic the real thing.

National health-care insurance, or its mandated provision, is unjust. It is nothing more than a forced charity, which is no charity at all. In this vein we might flatter ourselves into believing that we are doing good works, but it simply is not true. True mercy is extended as a matter of voluntary choice. It is not forced. Government mandates which require some to provide for others is false philanthropy. It is fundamentally selfishness unleashed and it will thwart future prosperity. If health insurance is extended the quality of medical care will decline. The end result will be exactly the opposite of what such schemes purport to offer. Instead of provision and prosperity, pain and hardship will follow.

---

1. Exodus 20:15.
2. Deuteronomy 27:17.
3. Frederic Bastiat refers to these two reasons for government involvement beyond its real purpose in *The Law* (Irvington-on-Hudson, N.Y.: The Foundation for Economic Education, 1950).
4. See Luke 4:1–13.

The Immorality of Social Security

by John Attarian

Social Security's defenders routinely laud it in moral terms, as "our most successful program of social reform,"[1] a humane, compassionate response to the needs of the elderly. One work puts it this way:

> None of us knows his or her fate. Today's good fortune can turn into tomorrow's disability. Most of us will gradually move from vigor to diminished capacity, and we will need help. All of us should ensure that such help will be there, just as we should extend help to those who need it today.
>
> The prime method of doing so is called social insurance. And the doing of it is called civilization.[2]

Social Security in other words, is part of what it means to be civilized and moral.

In truth Social Security's immorality is as monumental as its actuarial deficit, estimated under pessimistic assumptions at $23,188 billion as of January 1, 1994.[3]

To begin with, the system is, as Alf Landon described it in 1936, "a cruel hoax."[4] Social Security raises revenue by taxing worker incomes, then uses it to pay benefits to retirees, disabled persons, and other beneficiaries. Any money left after paying benefits and administrative costs is lent to the Treasury in return for special interest-bearing government debt, which can be redeemed as needed for money to pay benefits. Social Security, then, is a welfare program redistributing money from taxpayers to beneficiaries.

"Insurance"

Yet millions of Americans believe that Social Security is a retirement insurance program. They believe that the money they are

---

Dr. Attarian is a free-lance writer in Ann Arbor, Michigan. This article originally appeared in the January 1995 issue of *The Freeman*.

paying into it is being invested and will be paid back with interest when they retire. They believe that the benefit money belongs to them by right and that they have earned it. A letter to the *Wall Street Journal* expressed the view of many:

> . . . Social Security is not an entitlement program, but a savings system.
>
> When the government sends a Social Security check to an individual, it is not giving him anything; it is paying him back a portion of the money he has saved for his retirement through a special retirement plan. The money belongs to the individual, money owed to him, money systematically and forcibly taken from his paycheck as security against a time when he will be too old to work.[5]

Such misunderstanding (except the part about forcible extraction from one's paycheck) is the result of assiduous and dishonest use of insurance terminology by Social Security and its intellectual advocates. Its payroll taxes are euphemistically called "contributions."[6] The legislation authorizing them is titled the Federal Insurance Contributions Act (hence the acronym FICA).[7] Social Security's components are called Old-Age and Survivors' Insurance (OASI), Disability Insurance (DI), and Hospital Insurance (HI, or Medicare A). The *Social Security Bulletin* describes the program as "insurance," and its payments as "insurance benefits." A worker paying into the system is described as "covered" or "insured."[8] The Social Security Administration's free brochure *Understanding Social Security*, available at any Social Security office, assures readers that "we will honor your investment [sic] in Social Security."[9] It all sounds reassuring that one is doing something like buying a policy from Prudential or Mutual of Omaha.

Unfortunately for the hapless "covered workers" making their "contributions," *Understanding Social Security* doesn't tell them about *Flemming v. Nestor*, the 1960 Supreme Court decision by which the wife of a deported Communist lost her benefits, even though her husband had paid Social Security taxes. Didn't she have a legal right to those benefits, since her husband had paid those taxes? Not according to the Social Security Administration, which argued that:

> The OASI program is in no sense a federally-administered "insurance program" under which each worker pays premiums over

> the years and acquires at retirement an indefeasible right to receive for life a fixed monthly benefit, irrespective of the conditions which Congress has chosen to impose from time to time.[10]

The Court concurred: "To engraft upon the Social Security system a concept of 'accrued property rights' would deprive it of the flexibility and boldness in adjustment to everchanging conditions which it demands."[11]

Congress has already acted repeatedly with "flexibility and boldness in adjustment"—or, baldly put, cut Social Security benefits. Flexible and bold adjustments in 1977 and after included eliminating benefits for orphans and children of disabled or retired workers, who are full-time students and 18-21 years old; postponing cost-of-living adjustments (COLAs) for six months in 1983 and allowing future COLA delays under certain conditions; raising the retirement age (which deprives retirees of the benefits they would have collected had the earlier retirement age remained in effect); taxation of benefits (in effect a benefit cut); eliminating the minimum benefit under most conditions; and tightening the conditions for receiving lump sum death benefits.[12] So much for the pledge to "honor your investment."

Taxes versus Benefits

Social Security is disingenuous in another way about the relation between one's taxes and one's benefits. *Understanding Social Security,* i.e., the version of reality that the Social Security Administration produces for popular consumption, has it that the size of one's benefit depends on factors such as date of birth "and most important your earnings," and "In general, a Social Security benefit is based on your earnings averaged over your working lifetime."[13]

In reality, A. Haeworth Robertson, Social Security's Chief Actuary in 1975-1978 points out, "the relationship between taxes and benefits for an individual is so tenuous as to be virtually nonexistent."[14] This is because Social Security is a social insurance program, stressing "social adequacy." That is, "It pays benefits according to presumed need," and "no attempt is made to relate the benefits that a particular group of persons receives to the taxes paid by that group of persons to become eligible for such benefits." Two people in very different circumstances, say a married worker who dies leaving a wife and dependent children and a single worker who dies, may pay the same tax rates, yet the married worker's benefits will be much greater. While there is some indirect tie of taxes to benefits, it is "more tenuous than most people have realized, and this misunderstanding is an important factor in any public dissatisfaction with the Social Security system."[15]

Facing the Future

Similar deceit occurs regarding Social Security's future. *Understanding Social Security*, published in January 1994, opens by addressing the question "Is Social Security in Your Future?" and assures readers four times in three pages that "it will be there when you need it!"[16]

Yet for the past few years the annual reports of Social Security's Board of Trustees have warned that the system is not in close actuarial balance (i.e., projected future income doesn't match projected future cost) and that steps should be taken to strengthen the system and restore actuarial balance.[17] And just three months after the 1994 *Understanding Social Security* appeared, the trustees reported that the Disability Insurance trust fund is projected to run out in 1995, even under its optimistic economic and demographic assumptions. The Old Age and Survivors Insurance trust fund is projected to go broke in 2036 under the intermediate assumptions, in 2023 under pessimistic assumptions. Projected exhaustion dates for the combined funds (OASDI) are 2029 and 2014 under, respectively, intermediate and pessimistic assumptions.[18] These dates indicate considerable weakening in Social Security's position; the 1993 report projected OASDI exhaustion, for example, to occur in 2036 (intermediate assumptions) or 2017 (pessimistic).[19] Exhaustion of the Hospital Insurance trust fund, which pays Social Security's hospital benefits, is projected in 2004 under intermediate assumptions and in 2000 under pessimistic ones.[20]

And only actuaries and specialists know that Social Security's actuarial deficit, or excess of projected future costs over projected future revenues and trust fund assets, is soaring: under intermediate assumptions from $5,836 billion as of January 1, 1990, to $10,408 billion as of January 1, 1994; under pessimistic assumptions, from $14,282 billion to $23,188 billion.[21] Another indicator of Social Security's rickety long-term financial condition is its growing accrued unfunded liability. As of January 1, 1990, the unfunded liability for Old-Age and Survivors and Disability Insurance alone was $6,511 billion; four years later, it stood at $8,059 billion.[22] This is the amount of benefits that Social Security is liable to pay, but for which no money has been provided to pay them.[23]

This is the program that "will be there when you need it"?

As for the trust funds' assets, *Understanding Social Security* labels "false" the idea that the funds contain only "worthless IOUs" and asserts that Social Security's investment in government debt will be honored.[24] Alas, as former Chief Actuary Robertson acknowledges, "the trust fund assets have no tangible value [i.e., are worthless IOUs!] and represent only a claim on future federal revenue."[25] Social Security's investment will be honored only if the government forcibly extracts more resources from the private sector to repay it.

A private insurance company that took people's "contributions" for years; told them for years that they were "insured" with a "right" to benefits, without telling them it reserved the right to apply "flexibility and boldness in adjustment to everchanging conditions" if for some reason it couldn't pay them; lied to its "investors" about the value of its trust fund assets; and repeatedly assured them that their money "will be there when you need it" even while its own experts were forecasting oncoming financial ruin and calculating actuarial deficits and unfunded liabilities running into the trillions, would, rightly, be deemed unfair, untruthful in advertising, and fraudulent. "A cruel hoax," indeed. What then is the moral status of Social Security?

But even a private firm writing such a fraudulent prospectus has one moral advantage over Social Security: its victims participate of their own free will. Obviously, a financial system—especially an unsound financial system—which coerces people into it is morally inferior to a voluntary one.

Intergenerational Injustice

Social Security's coercive nature makes it inherently an engine of intergenerational injustice as well. It operates on a pay-as-you-go basis, meeting current expenses out of current revenues. Today's retirees are paid benefits with taxes levied on today's workers. That is, each generation is forced to support the previous generation, and as the program, and our population, have aged, the burden on each young generation has grown. And since the workers cannot leave the system their only hope of compensation for the injustice inflicted on them for the sake of their parents and grandparents is to have a similar injustice inflicted on their children and grandchildren.

This injustice is not altered by the trust fund surpluses which have accumulated since the 1983 tax increases. The only way the Treasury can get money to repay the bonds when Social Security presents them for payment, barring (unlikely) spending reductions elsewhere in the budget, is by extracting more resources from the workers by higher taxes or borrowing.

Social Security's intergenerational injustice could hardly be expected to endear the old to the young, and it hasn't. The Social Security literature speculates on a war—between the elderly understandably anxious for their benefits and the young groaning under a heavy payroll tax burden. The latter, some fear, may rebel at the prospect of the huge tax increases which will be necessary to pay the retirement benefits of the huge Baby Boom generation.[26]

This intergenerational discord is due to nothing else but Social Security's involuntary nature. No private retirement pension scheme ever has or ever could pit the generations against each other in a grim clash of interests, since private arrangements are entirely voluntary. Nobody ever heard the epithet "greedy geezer" when provision for retirement was one's own responsibility. Indeed, the better-funded a private pension fund is and the more lavish its benefits, the better off the young are, since their possible financial burden for the support of their parents is that much lighter. With Social Security, by contrast, the more the government tries to give the elderly or the better it tries to fund the program, the worse off the young are since they, not the earnings of private pension fund investments, are the sole source of financing.

The redistribution which Social Security carries out is likewise wrong. As a general rule, a person's earnings vary with his ability, enterprise, and industry, though unionization, nepotism, and other distortions might affect one's income. Social Security taxes are, ultimately, paid according to ability; the greater one's ability, the larger the amount of tax extracted. But, as we saw, benefits are paid according to "presumed need." That is, the program operates on the Marxist principle of "From each according to his ability, to each according to his need."

What of the argument that Social Security provides equity between generations? One is surely obligated to one's parents, and equity demands that one care for those who cared for one in one's childhood. But this hardly translates into perfect strangers having a moral claim on earnings forcibly extracted. And as Social Security's costs have risen, today's young generation faces a far heavier Social Security tax burden than previous ones, with ever-diminishing prospects of receiving benefits as lavish as those today's elderly enjoy. In truth, moral arguments about intergenerational equity run the other way: Social Security is inequitable to the young.

Perverse Incentives

But beyond the obvious wrongs which its mendacity and coercion entail, Social Security is evil in more subtle but nonetheless important ways, due to the perverse incentives which it creates and their impact on our national character and conduct.

For one thing, Social Security discourages savings and self-reliance. Believing themselves covered by the "savings" forcibly taken from their income, individuals save less than they would otherwise.[27] As a corollary it encourages irresponsibility and improvidence for the future. Social Security's huge size and longevity have made it a part of the landscape of people's thinking. For decades people have taken it for granted that much of the responsibility for their well-being in old age belongs to "society" or "the government." As President Grover Cleveland warned in 1887 when vetoing an appropriation for drought relief in Texas:

> the lesson should be constantly enforced that though the people support the Government the Government should not support the people. . . . Federal aid in such cases encourages the expectation of paternal care on the part of the Government and weakens the sturdiness of our national character.[28]

Still another sinister aspect of Social Security is its role in undermining the family. With Social Security assuming the responsibility for the elderly once borne by their children, both the ethos of reciprocal obligation between family generations and the incentive to marry and have children (to ensure care in old age) are weakened.

Finally, Social Security works insidiously against the value of life. Assuming that life is good and that a major purpose of human existence is reproduction—which, biologically speaking, it is, just as with all other living things—then it follows that other things being equal, that which encourages childbearing is good, and that which discourages it is not. As we saw, since much of the financial burden of caring for the elderly is now borne by Social Security and Medicare, the incentive to have children is thereby weakened. Moreover, as Allan Carlson of the Rockford Institute has observed, because struggling young couples are forced to participate in Social Security, they cannot improve their standard of living by reducing the support they give to the elderly. What they can do is delay or even forgo children. And in many cases they do; research across nations has found a causal connection between the size and generosity of a social security program and a country's fertility decline.[29] That is, social security has been a factor in the slow biological suicide of advanced Western societies.

Social Security can pay its current beneficiaries, and will be able to pay for some years yet. However, early in the next century, Social Security will face bankruptcy as the retiring Baby Boomer generation drives its costs above its revenues and exhausts its "trust funds" of Treasury debt. Radical reform, ideally privatization, will become urgently necessary. But should anyone attempt it, a firestorm of opposition grounded in morality will ensue. It will be one of the fiercest controversies of the future. Social Security, it will be argued, is moral, humane, compassionate, enlightened, progressive; radical reform is unthinkable, inhumane, callous, immoral. If needed reform is to be achieved, such objections must be overcome. And for that, it will be vital that the public realize just how morally flawed Social Security really is.

---

1. Senator Gaylord Nelson, "Foreword," in Robert M. Ball, *Social Security Today and Tomorrow* (New York: Columbia University Press, 1978), p. vii.
2. Merton C. Bernstein and Joan Brodshaug Bernstein, *Social Security: The System That Works* (New York: Basic Books, Inc., 1988), p. 288.
3. Sum of the Old-Age Survivors and Disability Insurance actuarial deficit of $6,964

billion and the Health Insurance actuarial deficit of $16,224 billion, both under pessimistic assumptions. Figures furnished to author by the Office of the Actuary, Social Security Administration, and Health Care Financing Administration, respectively. The actuarial deficit is the excess of Social Security's projected expenditures over its projected income and trust fund assets, over the next 75 years.

4. Quoted in Wilbur J. Cohen and Milton Friedman, *Social Security: Universal or Selective?* (Washington, D.C.: American Enterprise Institute, 1972), p. 7.

5. "It's Not an Entitlement: It's Money Owed to Us," in "Letters to the Editor," the *Wall Street Journal*, March 28, 1994, A13.

6. Social Security Administration, *Social Security Handbook* 1993, p. 482, *1994 Annual Report of the Board of Trustees of the Federal Old-Age and Survivors Insurance and Disability Insurance Trust Funds* [hereafter, *Annual Report OASDI*] pp. 30–32, 36, 38, 42, 48, 50, 63–64, 204–205, et al.; Robert J. Myers, *Social Security*, second edition (Homewood, Ill.: Richard D. Irwin, Inc., 1981), pp. 1, 5, 8–9, 27-30, et al.; M. C. Bernstein and Joan Brodshaug Bernstein, *Social Security: The System That Works*, pp. 16–17, 29, et al.

7. *Understanding Social Security*, p. 9.

8. *Social Security Handbook 1993*, pp. 25, 28, 192, 488.

9. *Understanding Social Security*, p. 5.

10. Peter J. Ferrara, *Social Security: The Inherent Contradiction* (San Francisco: The Cato Institute, 1980), p. 70.

11. *Ibid.*

12. A. Haeworth Robertson, *Social Security: What Every Taxpayer Should Know* (Washington, D.C.: Retirement Policy Institute, 1992), pp. 134–135.

13. *Understanding Social Security*, pp. 10–11.

14. Robertson, p. 68.

15. *Ibid.*, p. 195.

16. *Understanding Social Security*, pp. 4, 5, 6.

17. *1992 Annual Report, OASDI*, pp. 31–33; *1993 Annual Report, OASDI*, pp. 33–35; *1994 Annual Report, OASDI*, pp. 26–28.

18. *1992 Annual Report, OASDI*, p. 24.

19. *1993 Annual Report, OASDI*, p. 29.

20. *1994 Annual Report of the Board of Trustees of the Federal Hospital Insurance Trust Fund*, p. 3.

21. See footnote 3.

22. 1990 figure: Robertson, p. 116; 1994 figure, Office of the Actuary, Social Security Administration.

23. Robertson, p. 121.

24. *Understanding Social Security*, pp. 4–5.

25. Robertson, pp. 90–91.

26. See, e.g., Dorcas R. Hardy and C. Colburn Hardy, *Social Insecurity: The Crisis in America's Social Security System and How to Plan Now For Your Own Financial Survival* (New York: Villard Books, 1991), pp. 27–41.

27. Robertson, pp. 231–2.

28. *A Compilation of the Messages and Papers of the Presidents*, vol. XII (New York: Bureau of National Literature, Inc., 1897), p. 5142.

29. Allan Carlson, *Family Questions: Reflections on the American Social Crisis* (New Brunswick, N.J.: Transaction, Inc., 1988), p. 222.

INDEX

SUGGESTIONS FOR FURTHER STUDY

The following books from FEE are recommended to readers who wish to explore in greater depth the moral case for a free society.

Frederic Bastiat
The Law
A powerful summary of Bastiat's critique of socialism.
76 pages

Henry Hazlitt
The Conquest of Poverty
Capitalist production, not government programs, has been the real conqueror of poverty.
290 pages

The Foundations of Morality
The author presents a consistent moral philosophy based on the principles required for voluntary social interaction.
388 pages

Ludwig von Mises
The Anti-Capitalistic Mentality
A discussion of popular psychological arguments against capitalism.
114 pages

Human Action
Mises' magnum opus: a broadly philosophical work which is indispensable for scholars and students.
907 pages

J. Wilson Mixon, ed.
Private Means, Public Ends: Voluntarism vs. Coercion
A thought-provoking study of the virtues of private initiative and the failure of public administration.
230 pages

Edmund A. Opitz
Religion and Capitalism: Allies, Not Enemies
A profound discussion of the relationship of biblical religion to free market economics.
328 pages

Religion: Foundation of the Free Society
An anthology of Reverend Opitz's eloquent essays and articles.
272 pages

Hans F. Sennholz
Debts and Deficits
A devastating critique of our propensity to live beyond our means.
179 pages

Economic Commandments
A rational discussion of the Judeo-Christian foundation of the private property order.
47 pages

For current price information, or to request FEE's latest catalogue of more than 400 books on economics and social thought, write or phone:

The Foundation for Economic Education
30 South Broadway
Irvington-on-Hudson, New York 10533
(914) 591–7230; fax (914) 591–8910

About The Publisher

The Foundation for Economic Education (FEE) is a "home" for the friends of freedom everywhere. Its spirit is uplifting, reassuring, and contagious: FEE has inspired the creation of numerous similar organizations at home and abroad.

FEE is the oldest conservative research organization dedicated to the preservation of individual freedom and the private property order. It was established in 1946 by Leonard E. Read, and guided by its adviser, the eminent Austrian economist Ludwig von Mises. Both served FEE until their deaths in 1983 and 1973, respectively.

Throughout the years the mission of FEE has remained unchanged: to study the moral and intellectual foundation of a free society and share its knowledge with individuals everywhere. It avoids getting embroiled in heated political controversies raging in Washington; located in Irvington-on-Hudson, New York, FEE has always remained a purely educational organization.

We have a duty to speak and teach clearly and courageously. Our adviser, Ludwig von Mises, charged us at the conclusion of his great work on socialism:

> Everyone carries a part of society on his shoulders; no one is relieved of his share of responsibility by others. And no one can find a safe way for himself if society is sweeping towards destruction.
>
> Therefore, everyone, in his own interests, must thrust himself vigorously into the intellectual battle. None can stand aside with unconcern; the interests of everyone hang on the result. Whether he chooses or not, every man is drawn into the great historical struggle, the decisive battle into which our epoch has plunged us.

Hans F. Sennholz, President